LIFE SKILLS FOR TEENS

LEARN TO PREPARE FOR YOUR FIRST JOB, COOK A
GREAT MEAL, THRIVE IN COLLEGE, MANAGE YOUR
MONEY, COMMUNICATE FLAWLESSLY, PLUS
MUCH MORE

KYLA MILLER

CONTENTS

INTRODUCTION

As a teenager, life sure is confusing! For instance, why on earth were you given this book? After all, you're not completely clueless. Surely someone in your family should realize that you are a teenager and on your way to being a responsible adult.

What did they think when they bought this book for you? They are beginning to realize that you are getting to a point in your life where you are able to take on more responsibility. You've been given something that slaps - information. Yes, I hear you. You can google for the information you want. Just type in keywords and get pages of URL addresses with reams of facts and information. The question is, if you've never set up a home or lived on your own, how do you know which keywords to type in? Here's an example of what I mean. The car you've just bought has left a huge wet mark on the sidewalk. Typing 'stain on the sidewalk' in the search bar will give you plenty of suggestions on what to use to remove the stain, but none are helpful right now for figuring out what's actually wrong with your car and how to stop the ever-growing pool of liquid gathering there. However, turning to the chapter in this book on car maintenance and reading the list for troubleshooting car problems will be a quicker way to solve this urgent and immediate problem.

So, apart from sharing my hard-earned knowledge on how to maintain a car and do basic servicing and essential fixes, you will also learn how to cook basic meals that are nutritious, balance your money, and keep your home clean and tidy with the minimum amount of time spent, so you can still hang with your fam and post on social media. On the topic of social media, read through the chapter in this book on how to protect yourself against trolls. There are also tips to prevent you from getting stalked or scammed by weirdos.

Let me introduce myself and tell you why I have something to say that will be useful for you. Besides working as a teen mentor for almost a decade, my two daughters and son have put my suggestions into practice and are GOAT. I've helped teens with real-life problems and taught them essential life skills so that they could thrive as successful independent adults. I've had my own fair share of struggles similar to yours and have been where you are. I had to learn by trying and failing and trying again. Let me give you the shortcuts – the solutions that will save you pain and time.

Have you ever wished for plenty of money to buy whatever you want? Let me guide you through applying for a job, surviving the first few days at work, and making yourself a success. Read my tips on budgeting to make the most of your hard-earned cash.

Want to glow up next time you are given chores to do? Be the CEO of your own space? There are easy ways to manage your home space and impress with your cleaning hacks. Let me share what I have learned and help you do it the easier way.

Together we'll investigate some simple self-care tips and talk about making decisions and solving problems with win-win solutions. What about some pro tips on communicating with your family, roommates, and other adults in a way that they respect your opinion and actually listen to you? That would be an admirable skill to have! It's hard enough to talk to people you know; what about when you go to college later in the year? So, before you ghost me, read my secrets on engaging with fellow students, lecturers, and other aliens; just kidding! They are people just like you, and you're likely to find someone with common interests.

So, before you drag me with an 'Ok, Boomer', I'll give you a chance to start reading…

1

TASTY FOOD SKILLS

Whether you're staying home on your own while your parents are away, moving to college, or setting up your own home, you will have to eat. So, this is the starting point – the most important topic first. Food - how to get it, cook it, and make it taste great, together with some pointers on how to store it. After you've done takeout for two or three days, your budget will be blown, and you will want some variety and may even crave some green vegetables. There are many excellent cookbooks available with delicious recipes. Try one or two of these - *How-to Cookbook for Teens, The Complete Cookbook for Teens,* or *The Healthy Cookbook for Teens.* (All available on Amazon) Once you have mastered the basics, you can find other recipes online.

SHOP LIKE A CHEF

'Being a smart shopper is the first step to getting rich,' said Mark Cuban, the founder of the video portal Broadcast.com.

In a nutshell, what you want is the nicest-looking, best-tasting produce at a price that you can afford. It's a tall order but a good habit to form. Throwing away food that has gone off is like burning 'guap.'

Here is some strategy:

- Only buy what you know you'll eat.
- Plan your meals so that everything will be used up.
- Check the cupboards and fridge to see what you already have. Make a list of only the remainder of the items you will need.
- Make your own healthy snacks.
- Look for items on sale and adapt your menu plan to use them.
- Buy in bulk with ingredients that won't perish.
- Use basic ingredients that are cheaper.
- Cook in bulk and freeze the remainder.
- Compare the prices of items at different stores and then buy where you can get the best deal.
- Look for coupons or discount vouchers and use them.
- Check the high and low shelves in the store for cheaper brands and compare prices.

- Compare quantities for the best deal. Often single-serve sizes are more expensive than larger sizes.
- Check the shelf life or sell-by date on products to ensure you can use them before it goes off.
- Avoid unnecessary aisles and shop for only what's on your list. Aisles have indicator boards showing which products are displayed.

Reading dates on labels

There are usually two date indicators on labels:

Sell-by date: This tells the store manager when to pull products off the shelf. It also shows you when items are at their best. Often these items are marked down in price, and you can still buy them, but ensure that you can eat the food before the expiry date.

Expiry date: Always make sure that you have eaten the food on or before this date. Although some items can still be eaten a day or two beyond this date, they will no longer be at optimum freshness. You should throw risky foods such as meat, chicken, fish, dairy, and eggs away after this date.

The general rule for storing foods is FIFO – First in, first out. Make a habit of using up foods in the order you bought them, so your goods are always fresh.

Choosing the best

Here is a guide to buying the best produce on the super-market shelves.

Food	Good to buy	Avoid
Fruit	Plump well-colored flesh; Should yield slightly to gentle pressure if nearing ripeness	If dented or showing brown or soft spots or wrinkles on the skin
Vegetables	The skin should be firm and crisp	If wrinkled or limp
Herbs and salad greens	Crisp and plump leaves	If limp and yellowing
Chicken	Healthy-looking pink color	If yellowing or has a gray, greenish tinge
Fish	It has a sheen, and the flesh is opaque	No yellowing or dullness
Meat	Healthy darker pink color	Bones are yellowed or gray

Top Tip: How to check if an egg is fresh

Pour about 5cm/ 2 inches of water into a bowl. Place eggs into the water. Eggs that sink to the bottom and lay on their sides are fresh. Eggs that fall to the bottom but stand upright should be used within a day or two. Throw away any eggs that float to the top of the water level.

LET'S TALK ABOUT EQUIPMENT

To be efficient, quick, and safe in the kitchen, knowing the different types of equipment and their purposes will serve you well. When you plan to leave home and start setting up a kitchen of your own, you will find the list below extremely useful to help you decide what equipment to buy.

For slicing and cutting:

Chef's knife – Large bladed knife for general use. Cut meats and large hard-skinned vegetables.

Utility Knife – A slightly smaller blade used to slice smaller vegetables, fruit, chicken, and so on.

Paring Knife – Has a pointed tip and can be used for more precise cutting.

Bread Knife – Slices loaves of bread or bread rolls.

Kitchen Shears – Strong-bladed pair of scissors that can open the packaging and cut through chicken joints.

Steak knife – Used for cutting meat when eating at the table.

Vegetable peeler – Easily removes a thin layer of outer skin on vegetables and fruit.

Knife sharpener - Essential for keeping blades sharp and efficient.

From left to right: Paring knife, steak knife, Bread Knife, Utility knife, Chefs knife

Appliances:

Before using any appliances, read the instruction manual carefully and use the item only as intended. If you have misplaced the manual, you can find many instruction manuals on the internet if you have the appliance's model number.

Here are some general safety tips when using appliances:

Keep electric cords away from liquid because if electricity comes into contact with liquid, it can cause a short. Also, keep the plastic-coated cords away from the heated sides of appliances to prevent them from melting and causing a fire.

Close lids before switching appliances on to prevent the contents from splashing spectacularly around the kitchen.

Check the instruction manual for the use of various attachments and use the most effective one.

Microwave oven – You can use this appliance for reheating food, thawing frozen food, or cooking some foods such as vegetables, pasta, and sauces. The microwaves penetrate the food from all sides to a depth of about 4cm/ 1 ½ inch. Food should be stirred occasionally during cooking to spread the heat evenly and then allowed to stand for a few minutes to complete the cooking process.

Exact cooking times will vary depending on the wattage and capacity of your microwave. It is better to undercook the food, check, and add a little extra cooking time if necessary.

Use only suitable cookware such as glass and hardened plastic. Many plastic containers will say on them if they are microwave safe or not. Never use metal or tinfoil. Metal becomes too hot too quickly and will cause arcing and possibly a fire.

Cover the cookware while microwaving with a lid or plastic film with a small hole pierced in it to prevent splattering. You should pierce Any item with a skin or membrane. Prick the skin of potatoes and pierce the membrane of the yolk and white of an egg using the tip of a sharp knife.

Whether cooking, reheating, or defrosting, place thinner or smaller items in the center of the dish and thicker, larger items at the sides where the heat is stronger. Microwaves penetrate from the outside towards the inside. For example, when you warm a plate of steak and rice, place the rice more towards the center of the plate and the meat nearer to the edge. Arranging your dish in this manner will ensure that more heat penetrates the meat, which is thicker.

After each use, clean the microwave with a warm damp soapy cloth. Rinse with a clean cloth and dry.

Generally, food cooked in the microwave will take about 1/3 to 1/4 of the time it would take to cook in a standard oven.

Top Tip: Make popcorn in a microwave in just 2 minutes!

Mix about ¼ cup of kernels with a teaspoon of oil and some salt to taste. Pour into a microwave-safe container such as a pyrex dish and place a lid over it. There should be plenty of extra room for the kernels to pop. Microwave on full power for about 2 – 3 minutes or until you can no longer hear a popping sound.

Using oven gloves, take the bag out of the oven and open it very carefully to avoid being scalded by the escaping steam. Pour into a bowl and enjoy!

Toaster - To make crunchy toasted bread, select the setting you want, depending on whether you like your bread lightly toasted or dark and crunchy. Place slices of bread in the toasting compartments and switch it on by pushing the lever down. Most toasters will automatically pop the bread up when done. Allow slight cooling before removing to avoid burning your fingers.

If the bread is stuck, unplug the toaster and gently turn it upside down. If this does not work, gently dislodge using a plastic fork.

The crumb tray should be removed and cleaned out regularly to keep the toaster working efficiently.

Kettle – Use only for boiling water and never overfill. Some kettles switch off automatically when the water boils. Be very careful not to boil a kettle dry, as it will ruin the element and possibly cause a fire.

Instant pot – If you need to prepare food super-fast, cooking with pressure is the way to go. Read the instructions in the manual very carefully. Never overfill the inner pot, as too much pressure will build up. NEVER open the lid until the pressure is released and the valve is in the down position.

Some models can also be used as a slow cooker without the pressure, and you can cook cheaper tougher cuts of meat slowly until they are tender.

Air fryer – This is a healthy way of cooking food quickly because the fat drips off, leaving you with just nutritious food. It cooks bacon to a delicious crisp, but you can also use it for cooking chips, fish fingers, crumbed fish portions, chops, roast chicken, and roast potatoes.

Ensure that you engage the safety catch of the basket so that the base does not fall out when removing the basket. Use oven gloves when handling it, as it gets as hot as the conventional stove.

Hand Mixer – Use for quick mixing of batters, cake mixes, cream, and so on. Always insert the beaters; make sure that they are resting at the bottom of the bowl and that you firmly hold the machine before switching it on. Start with a slow setting and increase as the mixture begins to mix in to prevent dry ingredients from flying everywhere. When you have finished mixing, switch off while the beaters are still at the bottom of the bowl. Then lift the beaters and scrape off the mixture before removing them.

Top Tip

Sometimes when there is a lot of flour in the bowl, gently mix in the flour with a spoon before switching on your hand mixer to avoid that inevitable flour shower!

Clean the mixer immediately before the residue hardens. Unplug the machine from the wall socket and wipe it with a warm damp cloth. You can wash the beaters in hot soapy water and leave them to drip dry.

The two sets of beaters have different uses – the hooks are for dough, and the oval-shaped beaters are for cake mixes, eggs, and cream.

Stand Mixer – Use in the same way as the hand mixer. The only difference is that you don't need to hold the device while beating because it can be rested on a stand while working. Clean in the same way.

Blender – This is perfect for mixing smoothies, sauces, and soups. Never overfill the container. Place liquids in the container first and then add any dry ingredients. When using, ensure the lid is firmly in place and start with a low setting. Increase the speed as you need to. Many models have a pulse setting for better control.

Always clean immediately after using – half fill with warm water and add a few drops of dishwashing liquid. Ensure the lid is firmly in place and slowly switch to a low setting. Allow the water to blend and remove all the debris – pour the water out and rinse well. Turn upside down to drain well and dry. If necessary, you can use a bottle brush to help remove debris but never insert your fingers. Wash the lid in hot soapy water. Do NOT immerse the motor part to wash, but wipe it down with a hot soapy cloth and then dry it off. Use a Q-tip or old toothbrush to clean the control buttons.

Dishwasher - There is a trick to loading the dishwasher so that it works very efficiently. Ensure the water stream is not blocked, and remember to refill the salt and rinse aid compartments regularly. Scrape off excess food and if the items are very dirty, rinse briefly under running water. Load the machine as follows:

Top rack: Place glasses and cups upside down over the tines. Place small bowls on the top rack, and secure wine glasses in the slots for stems.

Bottom rack: Stack plates and bowls between the tines and place larger items at the edges, such as chopping boards. Dishwasher-safe glass mixing bowls and small pots can also be placed face down on the bottom rack.

Cutlery rack: Alternate forks, knives, and spoons in the cutlery caddy. Always point the blades of sharp knives down.

Add detergent in the correct place and select a suitable wash cycle. 'Fragile' for mostly glassware and 'heavy duty' for dirty pots and pans.

Unload the bottom rack first and then the top rack. Some dishwashers have a dry cycle as well. If not, you may need to dab water off the bottom of inverted cups.

Stove/Cooker – Many gas stoves have at least two types of burners - fast or high heat and slower or low heat. Read the instruction manual to see which burners are which. If you don't have a manual, you may be able to get one online if you type in the make and model of the stove.

Here is a guideline for using the burners:

High Heat: Use the fast, high-heat burners on the highest setting for bringing water or other liquids to a boil. You will see large rapid bubbles.

Medium-High Heat: This is usually around the three-quarter point on the dial or a 6/7 on an induction hob. The food will still cook quickly but will burn less easily. This is the most common heat setting for browning meat, sauteing vegetables, and frying. You will see small bubbles that rise rapidly.

Medium Heat: Set the temperature dial to around the halfway mark. This is a gentler heat for foods that need to cook until softer such as rice and vegetables. You will see large bubbles slowly rising as the food simmers.

Low Heat: Set the dial on the lowest temperature level to cook foods slowly for a long time. Cooking foods on low heat can also be referred to as simmering. This setting is ideal for soups and reducing and thickening sauces. You will see small bubbles rise occasionally.

Oven - Always ensure that the oven racks are evenly inserted and not at an angle—place items you wish to cook as centrally as possible. Before placing food inside, you should generally preheat the oven for 5 to 10 minutes. Check the food occasionally, but ensure you wear oven gloves and keep your arms away from the edges to prevent burning yourself. Here is a basic temperature guide for the oven.

Gas mark	Fahrenheit (°F)	Celsius (°C)	What this means	When to use
1	275	140	Cool	Warming foods Drying foods
2	300	150	Cool	Toasting nuts or oats
3	325	160	Moderate	Slow-cook meats or casseroles
4	350	175	Moderate	Most common temperature for baking roasts
5	375	190	Moderately hot	Some baking
6	400	200	Moderately hot	Scones, browning meat
7	425	220	Hot	Not recommended
8	450	230	Hot	Not recommended
9	475	240	Very hot	Not recommended

SAFETY FIRST

- The kitchen is one of the most dangerous places in the home. Make sure that you keep yourself safe by practicing the following:
- Never leave burners, cooking pots, and working appliances unattended.
- Keep the stove clean. Food debris and grease buildup can ignite and lead to a fire.
- Tie back long hair and roll up long sleeves.
- Wear non-slip footwear.
- If you smell gas, immediately shut off the emergency safety-stop valve. Open the window and doors to ventilate the kitchen and leave the room.
- Before lighting the oven, check that it is empty and the racks are in the correct position.
- Use burners on the back of the stove as much as you can.
- Only use pots that are appropriately sized for the burner.
- Do not leave an empty pan on a hot burner.
- Turn all pot and pan handles inwards or away from the edges where they can catch on loose clothes and be knocked off. If smaller children are around, they could grab the pot handle and pull the boiling liquid over themselves.
- Keep oven mitts, other cloths, and paper out of the way of the burners.

- Use oven mitts to remove pots and pans from the stovetop or oven.
- It is recommended to have a fire extinguisher, baking soda, and metal lids readily available in case of a fire emergency to extinguish flames quickly.

In Case of Fire:

Never use water on a grease fire. It is advisable to have a dry chemical fire extinguisher located near an exit so that in case of an uncontrollable fire, you can quickly evacuate the kitchen and the rest of the home while using the extinguisher.

- If the fire is confined to a small area, such as a pan, you can effectively put it out by pouring baking soda over it or placing a metal lid on top to smother the flames.
- It is important never to use flour or fan the flames when trying to put out a fire, as this can cause the fire to spread and become more intense.
- If the fire is in the oven, keep the door closed and turn off the heating element.
- Do not remove the lid or open the oven door until the pot or pan has completely cooled.

Cooking Equipment

Pots and Pans – Use small and medium-sized pots for general cooking unless you cook for a large crowd of friends. When starting to cook, you will need one saucepan, one medium-sized pot with a lid, one steamer, and one frying pan.

Many cooking pots have a Teflon coating. Use only Teflon or silicone utensils to stir and scrape inside the pot. If you use ordinary metal utensils, you will damage the Teflon coating. To clean, wipe out the residue with a paper towel and then use a hot soapy cloth to wash the inside. Wipe the outside as well. Then wipe out with a clean cloth and dry.

Other equipment

Cutting board - Use a cutting board when slicing food to prevent the knife from slipping, preserve the knife's sharpness, and prevent damage to kitchen counters.

Sieve or colander – This is especially handy for draining foods completely.

Can opener – Not all cans have pull-back tabs, so you will use this often.

COOK LIKE A PROFESSIONAL

Most recipe books give step-by-step instructions that you can easily follow. A good cookbook will also give you other information, such as the meaning of cooking terms and descriptions of ingredients. Before you start cooking, make sure that you have everything you need. Starting and then dashing to the shops usually doesn't end well. When you have used a recipe, make notes to remind yourself of any changes you made or want to make next time you cook. Maybe you would prefer to add more seasoning, or the quantity was too little to satisfy your appetite. This way, you'll quickly build a selection of 'go-to' favorite dishes.

Before starting to cook a new recipe, check the quantity. Often recipes are for four portions, so if you plan to cook only for yourself, you can do some math and divide everything by 4 (or by two if you are hungry), or you can cook the entire recipe and use the leftovers the next day.

HEALTHY EATING – IT'S YOUR CHOICE

Now, as teens, you have a whole life ahead of you, so it's worth making an effort to start getting into healthy habits from a young age. Once you get older, changing unhealthy eating habits gets much more challenging!

- Teens and young adults need extra nutrients to support bone growth, hormonal changes, and organ and tissue development, including the brain, so make sure that you get lots of vitamins and healthy fresh fruit and vegetables.
- Always eat breakfast.
- Drink plenty of water – 6 – 8 glasses a day.

- Limit highly processed food, sugary drinks, and junk food to only occasional treats.
- Healthy eating habits and physical activity can help lower the risk of obesity and all the health risks that come with it – diabetes, high blood pressure, etc. If your budget allows, it may be worth subscribing to a local gym, or a brisk walk is free and extremely good for you.
- Eating smaller meals spread out over the entire day is a healthier way to keep you satisfied. Here is a suggested meal plan for the day:

Breakfast - toast with egg *or* oats with cinnamon and honey *or* cereal and milk.

Mid-morning – fruit *or* cheese and biscuits *or* a small handful of nuts *or* yogurt and fruit.

Lunch – salad with a chicken sandwich *or* grilled fish and salad *or* soup and toast

Mid-afternoon – fruit *or* vegetable sticks and cottage cheese *or* oven-baked snacks.

Evening - meat/chicken/fish with mash/pasta, with carrots/peas/salad.

Note: If you are aware that you have special dietary needs, such as diabetes, or are gluten intolerant, make sure that you follow the eating plan given to you by a doctor or dietician. Any changes that you make to your diet should be discussed with your healthcare provider first.

Plan to have a variety

So, at this stage of your life, taking care of what you eat and watching your diet may seem unnecessary. But what you eat now will have a knock-on effect on your health later in your life. You only get one life, so make it a quality one you can enjoy. It just takes some planning to eat healthy food, and here is an outline:

You have probably heard of the food pyramid or 'healthy eating plate.'

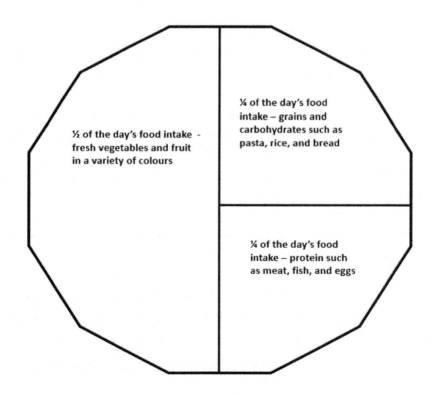

½ of the day's food intake - fresh vegetables and fruit in a variety of colours

¼ of the day's food intake – grains and carbohydrates such as pasta, rice, and bread

¼ of the day's food intake – protein such as meat, fish, and eggs

Half of your daily food intake should consist of fruits and vegetables. Select these foods in a rainbow of colors, including orange, yellow, red, green, purple, and white. Your daily food intake balance should be split between grains or carbohydrates such as whole wheat bread and pasta and proteins such as beans, meat, chicken, or fish.

Use only small quantities of olive or canola oil. In addition, you must drink at least 6 – 8 glasses of water per day. That means about 1.2 - 2 l per day.

Avoid snacking, but occasionally you can choose popcorn, nuts, dried fruit, or oven-baked snacks that will keep you satisfied for longer than oily fried and sugary foods.

General tips for healthy eating

- Grill, steam, or bake fish or meats
- Steam vegetables to retain the nutrients
- Use non-stick cookware to avoid using too much fat
- Except for baking, where quantity ratios matter, many recipes can be as successful using less fat and sugar.
- Reduce the amount of salt you use.
- Flavor foods using herbs.

Understanding food labels

An excellent trick to eating healthy is understanding the food labels on food packaging. You can often think a food is healthy until you read the label.

The following information is given on most food labels:

Serving size: This will give you an idea of how much of each food type you will eat. If the quantity is less than what you are used to, you will eat more and should recalculate the values given for the various foods. If the label tells you that there is 5g of fat in a 100 g portion, but you are eating 200g, then the fat content is 10g.

Calculate the total calories: Once you have checked the portion size, you can calculate the calorie or energy value. You can google how many calories you should eat in a day. The number of daily calories is determined by gender, height, weight, build or bone size, and activity level. Usually, teenage boys should have 2800 calories per day and girls 2200 calories per day.

Guidelines only: The information on the food labels is only a general guideline and should not cause you anxiety. There may be days when you are away and have to pick up takeout, and your daily intake exceeds the stated amount. That is okay so long as it is not the everyday pattern or continues for a long time.

Also, daily values are for food eaten over the entire day, not just for one meal. So split the recommended values and calories over 3 – 5 meals.

Know the nutritional terms:

Low calorie = less than 40 calories;

Low cholesterol = less than 2g of saturated fat;

Reduced = 25% less than the usual product

Good source of = at least 10 – 20 % of the daily requirement

Excellent source of = 20 % or more of the daily allowance

Calorie-free = less than 5 per serving

Fat/sugar-free = less than 1g per serving

No sugar added = the product may still have natural sugar but no extra has been added (So, fruit juice will be high in fructose but no extra sucrose has been added)

Low sodium = very little salt.

Get what you need

Choose foods with dietary fiber, potassium, vitamin D, calcium, and iron to keep yourself healthy.

Food labels must, by law, list the ingredients in the order of quantity if there is more than one ingredient. The ingredients that occur in the highest amount are listed first, and the others follow in descending order. This is valuable information if you are intolerant to substances or want to avoid ingredients such as sugar, salt, or fat. Most foods have 'hidden sugars,' which provide little nutritional value but push up your daily intake of calories.

Why should you avoid junk food?

Many readily available foods are often designed to fill you quickly rather than provide good nutrition. Your body naturally prefers a balance of nutrients that cannot be gained from junk food. While the odd treat won't do too much damage, constant and regular eating of these foods will have long-term effects on your health for these reasons:

- Blood sugar quickly spikes and then drops, leaving your body depleted of energy.
- Blood pressure can be raised due to high levels of sodium
- Manufactured additives such as MSG can lead to an increase in inflammation levels in the body.
- Your nutritional intake is compromised - if you feel full and satisfied after a junk meal, you're unlikely to want to eat fruit or vegetables which contain essential nutrients.
- Dietary fiber is lacking – most junk foods are served with refined carbohydrates. A lack of dietary fiber can lead to digestive tract problems.
- Junk foods can cause binge eating.

To get started, you can try these easy and tasty recipes:

Quick and easy Omelets (for 1)

2 eggs

1 tablespoon milk

Salt to taste

Pepper to taste

Small block 3x3x3 cm cheese, grated (or more if you wish!)

Filling:

1/2 small tomato, chopped

1/4 small onion, chopped

2 chives chopped

Optional: chopped green or red pepper, mushrooms, parsley, garlic, leftover bacon, chopped ham

Lightly fry the ingredients for the filling until just cooked.

Beat together eggs, milk, salt, and pepper until the eggs are frothy. Pour into a heated, lightly oiled, or non-stick pan. Cook over medium heat until the edges start to curl away from the sides and the top is almost set. Gently turn the omelet over using a large spatula or egg lifter. Allow the other side to brown and set.

When done, place the omelet on a plate with the filling on one half of it and fold it over. Sprinkle grated cheese on the top.

Mock Pizza Breads (for 1)

2 slices seeded bread

2 tablespoons tomato sauce or relish

2 slices ham

Half a cup of grated cheese

Sprinkle of herbs

Spread one side of the bread with tomato sauce or relish. Place 1 slice of ham over the sauce. Sprinkle cheese on top, and then sprinkle the herbs on top. Place the 'pizza slices' at the bottom of the basket in the air fryer. Set the air fryer to 180 deg C and cook for 3 - 5 minutes until hot and the cheese melts. Remove very carefully with a spatula.

Top Tip

Save money by buying cheaper cuts of meat and tenderizing them in baking soda and water for thirty minutes before marinating.

STORING FOOD SAFELY

Some foods deteriorate quickly if not stored properly. Eating food that is 'off' can cause you to get sick. At best, you may vomit or get diarrhea; worse, you may get food poisoning and need to be hospitalized. High-risk foods are chicken, fish, dairy, meat, and eggs. The risk is even higher when these foods are still raw.

Food that has been thawed should never be refrozen. If the food thawed while raw, cook it first before refrigerating.

It would be best if you kept the fridge at 5°C/40°F or below and the freezer below -18°C/0°F.

As soon as you return from buying food at the store, pack food away.

Tins and sealed packages - can be kept in a cupboard

Fresh vegetables and fruit – store in a fridge. Exceptions are potatoes, onions, butternut, gems, citrus fruit, and avocado, which you can keep at room temperature.

Dairy products and eggs - keep in the fridge.

Meat, chicken, and fish – Freeze and keep for less than six months.

Goods bought in a frozen state must be taken as quickly as possible straight into the freezer at home. If they thaw, you must cook them first before storing them.

Cooked leftover foods should be placed in an airtight container and kept in the fridge for no longer than two days. Clear out any leftovers in the refrigerator at least once per week and if not yet eaten, throw them away.

Here is some information to use as a guide:

Apples – Keep in the fridge for 1 - 2 weeks. Can be frozen if you cook them first, then use them for sauce or desserts.

Apple and other juices - 1 week to 10 days in the fridge.

Apricots – Keep for 1 – 2 weeks in the fridge. Freezing is not recommended.

Avocado Pear - Keep at room temperature until ripe.

Bananas - Keep at room temperature until ripe.

Bacon – Keep in the fridge for 1 -2 days. Can be frozen for 1 – 3 months.

Beans, Green – Keep in the fridge for 1 week or freeze for 1 -3 months.

Bread – Keep in an airtight container for 1 day, in the fridge for 2 -3 days, or freeze for up to 1 month.

Broccoli – Store in the fridge for 1 -2 weeks or freeze but use after 1 – 3 months.

Butternut – Store unpeeled at room temperature, after peeling keep in the fridge for up to 1 week or freeze for 1 -3 months.

Chicken, raw and ground – Keep in the fridge for a maximum of 1 -2 days, or freeze for up to 3 - 4 months.

Chicken, raw whole – Keep in the fridge for 1 – 2 days or freezer for up to 9 months.

Carrots - 1 - 2 weeks in the fridge, 1 – 3 months in the freezer.

Cucumber - Keep in the fridge for up to 1 week. Freezing is not recommended.

Eggs - 1 - 2 weeks in the fridge but freezing is not recommended.

Grapes – Keep in the fridge for up to 1 - 2 weeks. Freezing is not recommended

Lettuce – Will keep fresh in the fridge for 1 - 2 weeks, freezing is not recommended.

Meat, raw ground meat & hamburgers – Keep in the fridge for 2 days, and 3 - 4 months in the freezer.

Meat, raw steaks, chops & roasts – 3 - 5 days in the fridge and 4 - 12 months in the freezer.

Milk - 7 days in the fridge, up to 1 month in the freezer.

Oranges - Store at room temperature.

Pears - 1 - 2 weeks in the fridge or cook and then store in the freezer using in sauce or desserts.

Potatoes - Store at room temperature.

Strawberries - Keep in the fridge for up to 1 week.

Tomatoes – Keep in the fridge for 1 - 2 weeks, cook before or after freezing, and use in sauces or stews.

You probably feel like this is an overload of information. You will cope – just take this step by step, starting with planning what to eat for the next few days. Follow the meal suggestions under the healthy eating heading. Next, make a shopping list and shop for the food you need. Store the foods following the guidelines in this chapter. Next, look at the info on what you'll need to prepare meals and how to use the cooker and appliances. You can follow the recipes we have given you and have fun preparing your first meal. Then when your stomach is full, you'll be able to cope with the next steps. You may even be 'shook' at your skills.

2

MAKING YOUR MONEY WORK
FOR YOU

Managing money may be a new concept for you and seem a little daunting. Here is some basic information that will help you get to grips with how to use it, get what you need, and grow it by saving and investing. Let's start at the beginning...

WHAT IS A BUDGET?

It is a simple plan to spend your money without exceeding your income, so you still have some money to save for the things you want.

Sounds simple? Well, actually, it really is simple. There are many budgeting apps and templates available. Read reviews and then download one that you think will work for you. Everyone's income looks different. Some are lucky enough to have a fixed income, while others have a variable income. What you need is something that helps you record your income and allows you to set up various categories to plan how much to spend on the things you regularly need and what you will be saving for the things you want.

Once you have set up a budget, please make up your mind to stick to it rigidly. Here is an example of a simple monthly budget. You can change the categories and amounts to suit your situation:

Income:

Salary $3 000,00

Other $800,00 from part-time work

Total: $3 800,00

Minus the Expenses:

Savings long-term Retirement $500,00

Savings – short-term for travel/holiday $760,00

Savings Urgent unplanned events $550,00 (variable)

Rent $620

Car payment $450,00

Gasoline $120,00

Car Insurance $41,40

Student loan payment $61,20

Utilities - gas/water $152,50

Mobile phone $6,00

Health Insurance $83,00

Clothing account $110,00

Food $210,00

Entertainment $122,50

Charity $5,00

Total: $3 791,60 – Should be less than the Income.

Working out a budget in 6 easy steps:

Record your income after taxes and compulsory deductions: Use the amount that actually lands in your bank or your pocket. If you earn a salary, your employer will have to deduct and pay over the taxes or any other amounts required by law before you get a cent. These deductions should reflect on your payslip issued at the end of every month or week, depending on when you get paid. If you work part-time, you will have to keep track of your income and the tax you need to pay.

1. *List your fixed expenses:* These are rent, car payments, student loan repayments, mobile phone rental, gym

subscription, and so on. The amount stays the same month to month, and you know what to pay.

2. *Next, list your variable expenses:* These are items such as food, entertainment, clothes, etc. The amounts may vary from month to month.

3. *Then, list your savings goals:* There should be at least two savings goals: a long-term retirement goal and a short-term savings goal. Okay, let's discuss this! Retirement may be something like 45 years away but trust me unless you start now, you will be hungry and homeless once you can no longer work. A small amount of money saved consistently over a very long time will amount to much more than if you try to play catch up ten years before you have to retire. The other savings goal is short-term, such as 1 – 3 years, and will be for something you really want. Maybe you would like to take three months off work and travel. Or, you would like to own a car and need to save for a down payment.

4. *Add the figures:* The fixed income amounts are easy to fill in. Now, put estimated amounts next to the variable costs. Here you will need to do some research or work out through trial and error to get totals. Do rough calculations on how much you will need to spend on three meals a day for 30/31 days in a month or seven days if your budget is a weekly budget. Consider revisiting and adjusting these amounts as you test out the budget. Next, you need

to add up all the expenses and add in the amounts that you want to save. Check that the expenditure does NOT exceed the income. If it does, go back and re-evaluate and adjust the variable costs or the savings amounts. It's okay to start by saving only small amounts and increase this later as your income grows.

5. *Determine that you will stay within your budget:* This is about attitude and determination. If you get into the habit of working strictly within your budget and not spending more money than you earn, you will avoid getting into a debt trap. Once you are in debt, it is very difficult to get out of it.

The amount you can save each month will depend on your income and total expenses. It would be best to plan to save at least 10% of your income but aim for more. The more you save each month, the more you will have to cope with unplanned expenses that often crop up.

Top Tip

Try to cut something small from your budget that you can do without. Even something that only costs you $30 a month saves $360 a year. It all adds up!

OPENING A BANK ACCOUNT

Let's start by understanding the general financial terms used by bankers and financial professionals. This will help you navigate through what can be a confusing area of adult life.

Beneficiary – The person to whom you will be paying money.

Cheque (UK) or check (US) – A form indicating to the bank to pay the person you have named with the amount that you have filled in. Many banks are no longer using these, and more and more banking is being done via apps or EFT (Electronic Funds Transfer).

Credit – if you make a payment to an account, it reflects as a credit. 'Credit' can also be a loan from the bank in the form of a credit card, etc. So, the bank gives you money upfront to buy something, and then you have to pay them back over a period of time. Be cautious of doing this, as you will be charged interest on what you loaned.

Deposit – Put money into a bank account.

Gross income – The amount you are paid before any deductions are made.

Interest – The bank gives you a small amount of money each month to invest with them. This varies depending on the type of account and how much money you have invested. Interest rates vary and link to the Prime Rate your country's reserve bank sets. It's always a good idea to research the prime rate to know whether your bank is giving you a fair amount of interest.

You will also be charged interest if you take a loan from the bank.

Investment – Putting your money into the bank is an investment because it earns some interest. You can also invest in stocks or companies.

Net income – The amount of money you are left with after deductions.

Service charge – Sometimes, the bank will take a small amount off your account each month to cover their costs.

Withdraw – To take money out of a bank account.

Now that you understand some basic terms, you can decide which bank to use. Your choice will depend on the following:

- Which bank is closest to where you live or work? Although most banking gets done online or through mobile apps, you may need to visit your branch from time to time, so it makes sense to use a bank nearby.
- Which bank offers you the best rate? Some banks offer special deals for students, such as no service fee, easy application for a study loan with low-interest rates, and extended repayment time.

- Some banks offer home loans at slightly less than the prime rate. If you are paying a home loan over 20 years, ½ % can significantly affect the interest you will pay.
- Convenience is key – some banks have better apps or are easier to use online.
- Ensure that the bank you use is an accredited financial services provider, FDIC (US), or FSCS (UK)-insured. This scheme protects you from losing up to a certain amount if the bank you deposited in has failed.

In short, choose a bank that can give you the best service at the lowest rate but pays the best interest.

To open a bank account, you must visit your nearest branch with government-issued identification such as an ID card, social security number (US), National Insurance Number (UK), passport, or driver's license. You will also need to deposit a minimum amount of cash into the account to open it. If you are over 18, you can do this by yourself; otherwise, you will need a parent to accompany you.

Once you have opened the account, ask to be linked online or on a mobile app. Some banks allow both, but others want you to choose which method you want to use. Make sure you change your passwords regularly and check your bank statement often to ensure that no one has hacked into your account. If you don't recognize transactions, notify your bank immediately.

Dealing with unknown transactions can be a headache, but this one takes the cake. A man was accidentally charged a whopping 23 quadrillion dollars on his debit card due to a technical glitch. And as if that wasn't enough, he didn't have the funds to cover it, resulting in a costly overdraft fee of $15!

Top Tip

Secure your online and app banking portfolios against fraud. Never give out your password or PIN to anyone.

Various Bank accounts:

Current or cheque/ checking account – You can often transact by depositing and withdrawing money, but the interest paid to you will be low. You will be issued a card and a PIN (Personal Identification Number). Remember to change your PIN to something you can easily remember, but no one else will easily guess. Never store your PIN together with your card because this increases the chances of thieves being able to take all your money if your card is lost or stolen.

Savings account – For depositing money, you will not draw out unless there is an emergency. The interest paid to you is slightly higher.

Money Market/ call account – These accounts generally pay higher interest as you agree to leave your money there for longer. You must give a certain period of notice to the bank if you are going to withdraw money. This is a suitable type of saving account if you are saving for something specific, like a car.

Fixed deposit or Certificate deposit– You can deposit a fixed amount each month but cannot draw out money for a negotiated period, usually three years or more. The interest paid to you is the highest that the banks can pay and depends on the amount in the account.

Credit Cards – Before you can get a credit card, you will need to build up some banking history or credit score. The bank wants to know if you are responsible with your money and will pay back the loan as agreed. With a credit card, the bank advances money up to an agreed amount, and you pay them back over an agreed period. Unless you pay back the balance in full before interest is added, this is not a wise way of using money, especially for everyday expenses. Spending can quickly get out of control, the interest charged is high, and it is difficult to get out of debt and keep up the repayments.

Take a lesson from Tyler, who, shortly after he started working, got himself into debt by loaning money from people so that he could buy expensive furniture for his studio apartment. He first realized he had made a big mistake when four months later, he ran out of money to purchase food two weeks before payday, and he constantly got calls asking where the loan repayments were. Fortunately, his friend Kyle noticed that he was seriously anxious and, after talking to him, showed him how to draw up a budget, working on an amount each month to pay off the loans. Next, Tyler had to call the people he had loaned money to explain how much he could repay each per month and work out a deal. For the next six months, he had no money for takeout or entertainment, but he stuck to the plan and paid off every cent. If you were to meet Tyler and talk to him, his advice would be: Don't borrow money to buy things you can live without. Save until you can afford them and stay out of debt.

Using the ATM

The bank will issue you a bank card that you can use to pay at the shop's cashier or checkout counter. You can also use it to draw cash. When using your card, be aware of your surroundings and ensure it is safe to use without interference. Never allow anyone to see your PIN when you enter it.

1. Insert the card at the ATM, follow the prompts to enter your PIN, and select which account you want to use.
2. Enter the amount that you wish to withdraw.
3. Quickly store the cash in a wallet or purse and make sure that you retrieve your card and the receipt.

4. Never allow anyone to stand close to you when using the machine or to see your PIN. If you need help, go into the bank to ask a bank employee to help.

The ATM can also be used to check your balance and to get a mini statement.

To transfer money or pay online

Step 1: Log into your bank's website and select the 'online banking' function.

Step 2: Log into your banking profile with your username and password. (The username is issued by the bank when you open the account and set up your online banking profile.)

Step 3: Choose the payment option such as 'pay' or 'transfer.'

Step 4: Load the beneficiary by entering the account number, the name of the account holder, and the sort code (UK) or Routing Number (US). For international payments, you will need the IBAN/BIC Number of the person to whom you are making the payment to.

Step 5: After successfully loading the beneficiary, you can select this account to pay. Enter the amount that you want to pay and type in the references. Your reference will appear on your bank statement and help you identify who was paid. The beneficiary reference is the one that will appear on the other person's bank statement. This should help them identify the payment as yours - your invoice number, account number at the store, or your name. Avoid generic or vague references such as 'monthly payment' – they may have thousands of people paying and need something specific to identify that you have made the payment into their account.

Example of a debit card

Front of card:

1. Bank logo and name are displayed.
2. Date on which the card must be renewed.
3. Your personal bank card number.
4. Your name.

5. Black magnetic strip which 'talks' to the point of sale machine and collects the retailers bank details.

6. White stripe for your sample signature.

7. Bank contact details.

8. The 3- or 4-digit number is your security number, also known as the CVV/ CVC number. It is used to verify your card details when buying online or through an app. It acts as a security feature. Online orders can only be done if the person ordering has the physical card in their hand. This is why it is essential to make sure that no one has access to your card to prevent them from ordering goods against your account.

9. Many cards also have a hologram placed either on the front or the back of the card. This is an additional security feature because holograms are very difficult to fake.

10. A unique smart chip containing a microprocessor which codes each transaction and helps to keep your card safer from fraud.

Example of a Cheque/Check

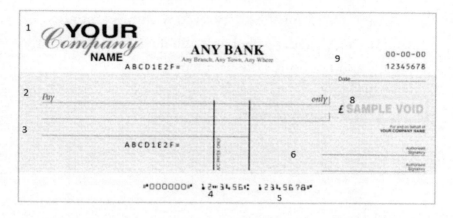

Although not many banks still use cheques/checks, it is included here so that you can see what it looks like if you happen to get one. The following information is found on the cheque/check:

1. The name of the company or person issuing the payment.
2. The name of the person who should receive the payment.
3. The amount of the payment in words. This must match the digits at 8.
4. The unique number of the cheque.
5. The bank account number of the person/company making the payment.
6. The signature of the person issuing the payment.
7. Second signature if a company requires two people to sign cheques.

8. Amount to be paid in digits. Must match words at 6.
9. The date on which the payment was issued. The Cheque/check must be deposited within six months of it being issued, or the bank will declare that it is 'stale' and not honor the payment.

How to read a bank statement:

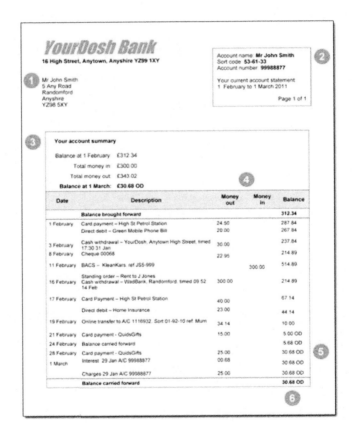

The information that you will find on a bank statement is as follows:

1. Your name and address
2. Your account name, number, and details,
3. Dates to which this statement is relevant
4. Two columns of figures appear – the left column is the debits or the money that has gone out of the account, either by withdrawing cash or by paying for goods bought or accounts paid. The right-hand column shows credits or amounts of money that you or others have paid into your account. Anyone can pay money into your account if they have your account details, but no one should be able to withdraw money other than yourself. The only exception to this is if you have signed a debit order/direct debit agreement authorizing a company to deduct payment regularly. Check these transactions carefully to ensure that the correct amount is always deducted.
5. The figures in this column show the balance in your account after the transactions are done and will fluctuate as deposits are added, and withdrawals or payments are subtracted.
6. The final balance or amount in your account at the time the statement is printed or issued.

Debit Cards versus credit cards

With a debit card, you can only spend the money you have already deposited into the account. With a credit card, the bank advances money to you up to a specifically agreed total. You use the bank's money to pay for goods and then pay the bank back with interest added on.

Should you get a credit card?

You will have to be 21 to apply for a credit card. Generally, it is best not to have a credit card. However, there are some advantages to having a credit card. Some banks offer free travel insurance if you purchase air tickets with a credit card, which can save you a lot of money. If you have a sudden emergency, such as a broken tooth, you can use a credit card to pay and then spread the repayments over a few months, depending on what you can afford to repay. The longer you take to pay back, the more interest you will pay. Never use a credit card to buy everyday items such as food or clothes. It is challenging to keep track of how much you spend with a credit card, and very easy to overspend, thinking that you have plenty of time to pay back. You will be charged interest on an outstanding balance, meaning you pay more for items than if you paid cash or with a debit card.

YOUR CREDIT SCORE

A credit score is a number that represents how trustworthy you are with borrowing and repaying the money. Lenders, like banks and credit card companies, use credit scores to decide whether to give you a loan or credit card and at what interest rate. You will need to build a good credit score, starting now while you are young. This is possible if you manage your money responsibly and pay your bills promptly. A good credit score allows you to borrow money if you need to later when you want to buy a house or get a credit card. You can also save money by getting cheaper insurance or lower lending interest rates. You can check your credit score by using websites such as Experian. A good credit score will be 670 or higher.

Build a good credit score by paying your bills on time, catching up quickly with past-due accounts, paying extra amounts into your accounts if you can, and limiting the number of loans you apply for.

It is easier to build a good credit score than to reverse a bad score, so develop the habit of paying accounts on time and being responsible with your money.

SAVING AND INVESTING

If you budget your income carefully, you should be able to pay for the essentials you need and still have some money left to save or invest.

Saving is a safer way of growing your money. You put money into a secure account, where it can gain interest and grow.

Investing money is similar but riskier because you put money into stocks and shares or lend it out to get back more. You are putting your money into something that can only estimate growth in the future. Although calculations of interest are done using formulae and predictions based on historical data, no one can predict the future. Hence, growth and interest rates are estimates that may or may not yield the hoped-for amounts. Example: A start-up company needs capital to get off the ground, and you invest money. They estimate that quick sales over two years will double your initial investment. The company may be a fantastic success, and you get an excellent return on your investment, or it may be a failure, and you will lose all your money. There is no guarantee.

Before investing money in anything, do your research well, and don't allow yourself to be swayed by promises of quick or big money. Check out a company's past performance and read current news articles to keep up to date with factors that could affect business, such as politics, inflation, natural disasters, etc. These can all affect the performance of companies and the amount of money they make. Taking calculated risks can lead to exciting opportunities and rewards, but it's important to research and think carefully before making any decisions that could have long-term consequences.

NEEDS VERSUS WANTS

Needs are the items that you must have to survive: food and water, electricity/gas, a basic wardrobe of clothes, and a place to live. Other essential items are transport to get to work and, depending on your country, possibly medical insurance.

Wants are items that you would like to have but can live without if you don't have them.

Top Tip

Try the 30-day money challenge: For 30 days, only buy what you need and put off any purchases you want. At the end of the month, you can use the money you saved to buy things you still want. This challenge can help you save money by avoiding impulsive purchases.

KEEPING RECORDS

Keep all paper or communication relating to money in a logical order, where you can find information if you have to. Paperwork can either be filed or scanned and saved. Label folders (paper or digital) according to the categories you have set up in your budget template. Always keep receipts or proof of payment when paying for items. If there is a query or your payment was misallocated, you will have proof that you paid. Keep invoices and pay slips, so you can see what money came into your bank account and what was spent.

These documents should correspond to your bank statement, and you should be able to identify each transaction on your statement. If not, query the statement with the bank.

You should keep records for 5 -7 years in case a bank or the Tax Services want to query your money affairs.

Also, keep a copy of your rental agreements, home lease, and insurance policies. File these neatly labeled in a folder where you can easily find them.

Top Tip

Before you sign any documents, ensure you have read the entire document and understand what you are signing. If you do not understand something, ask for an explanation.

WHY SHOULD I GIVE TO CHARITY?

There are many organizations that help people who have disabilities, are orphaned or are simply unable to work for various reasons. Many charities also help animals that need to be taken care of. Before you give money to a charity, research to ensure that the charity is registered as a Non-Profit Organization (NPO). You also need to ensure that the money they receive is used for the purpose they claim. Bona Fide charities are open about financial matters and will display annual reports on their website. Choosing a cause can be confusing as there are so many. Think about where your compassion lies – with orphaned children, abused women, substance-dependent teenagers, people with disabilities, or homeless animals.

Donations can be monetary, and you may get a tax rebate for your contribution. You can claim a tax deduction in the USA if you donate to a 501(C)3 registered organization. You must also file a Schedule A with your tax form. In the UK, When individuals donate money to charity or community amateur sports clubs (CASCs), they do not have to pay taxes on that money. This is called tax relief.

Donations do not need to be in the form of money. You can also donate your time by volunteering to do required tasks – painting, shopping, keeping people company, extra lessons to orphans, cleaning out animal shelters, walking dogs, etc. The possibilities are endless.

Another way of helping a charity is by donating unused goods, such as clothes, furniture, books, stationery, etc. Always make sure that the items are in good condition and clean. Broken items are of no use.

Protect yourself from scams:

- Do thorough research to verify that the charity is a valid organization.
- The charity must be registered on the IRS database as an NPO to qualify for a tax deduction.
- Don't allow yourself to be manipulated into giving or giving more than you want to.

- Never give cash, but rather pay by cheque, card, or EFT.

Determine today to be disciplined with spending money and keeping accurate records. You will experience less stress and anxiety if you can buy or pay for your needs. Enjoy the rewards of saving to occasionally buy items or do the things you really want to, and watch your money grow with wise investments.

3

GAIN THE RESPECT YOU WANT

J.K Rowling, the author of The Harry Potter stories, said, "A good first impression can work wonders." It's unfortunate but true that people will evaluate you based on what they first see. The good news is that you can influence that first impression. Write down three words to describe what you would like people to think when they first meet you. Then, with the information in this chapter on clothing and personal grooming, you can make your choice of first impression a reality.

GETTING CLOTHES TO FIT

It's not YOUR body that doesn't fit store-bought clothes – it's the clothes that don't fit you. It's a fact that there is no global benchmark for sizing in the fashion industry and so it is rare to find clothes that fit perfectly all the time. What one retailer calls a size 12, another labels size 10, while it actually only partially fits a size 14 body. Yes, it's complete chaos, complicated by the fact that there are a variety of styles, some close fitting and others meant to hang loosely. So how do you get clothes to fit correctly to create that positive first impression to gain respect?

Start by taking your measurements - This can be tricky to do on your own, so get someone to help and use a dressmaker's tape measure. The men will need to measure around their neck, chest, waist, hip, and down the inseam of trousers (from the top of the thigh to the ankle, measured on the inside of the leg). The ladies will need to measure the bust, waist, and hip.

Check the retailers' size chart – Ignore labels for now, but find your measurements on the sizing chart in-store or on the store's website. Choose the size that covers most of your measurements or the size that caters to your largest measurement. This is likely to be the correct size for you. You may still need to go to a tailor or dressmaker to get some alterations done. This was a tip that my friend Courtney was given by one of her work colleagues. So, when she found a blouse that fitted her at the bust and hips, but the waist was too big and baggy, she bought it and then went to a dressmaker to take the waist in. Now the blouse fits her perfectly. Her friend Lloyd purchased a pair of trousers that fit really well on the hip. He liked the style and color, but the trousers were too long at the inseam. When he told the shop assistant, she offered to send the trousers to their alterations department so that a tailor could shorten the legs of the trousers.

We are all shaped differently, so next time you go to the mall to buy clothes, check the following areas to make sure that a garment fits:

- Close the button at the neckline of a shirt or blouse. You should not feel choked but be able to put two fingers between the collar and your neck comfortably.
- The top of the sleeve should start at the end of your shoulder line. If the shoulder seam hangs down (unless the style is meant to be a 'drop shoulder style'), you need a smaller size. A correctly fitted shoulder is essential for tailored jackets. The shoulder seam should also not look too narrow. In this case, take a larger size.
- For shirts and blouses, the button at the largest part of the chest/bust should not be strained or pulling the buttonhole open. If you pinch the center front at this point between your thumb and forefinger, you should be able to gather about half an inch of fabric.
- The waist must be comfortable. It is too tight if the waistband cuts into your body or makes you look like a muffin sitting on top of the paper casing. On the other hand, if you need to wear a belt and there

are folds in the waistband when the belt is buckled up, the waist is too large.

- Always sit and bend down when you fit clothes. If the garment strains across the hips, or you can't bend down or sit, you need a larger size. Imagine sitting on the office chair all day in the garment. If that seems like an uncomfortable thought, try a larger size.

- Hems should reach where they are intended – above the knee, at the ankle, or an inch above the ground. The hem can usually be shortened if necessary but not lengthened.

Most fitting rooms have multiple mirrors so that you can see how the garment fits from the side and back. The basic line of the garment should skim your body but not restrict your movement or cause bulging. If you are unsure about the fit, ask about the return and refund policy. If the garment can be returned, you can always do so after a friend has given you an honest opinion. Don't be shy to thank the assistant politely and walk out, without having bought anything – it's important only to buy clothes that fit well.

Top Tip

If you struggle consistently across all stores to find clothes that fit well, then rather get yours custom-made by a tailor or a dressmaker.

If you have bought clothes online and the garment does not fit when you check the above points, either package it up and send it back to get a refund or have a tailor or dressmaker alter the garment to fit better.

Wearing clothes that fit well will boost your confidence and get you respect. When buying clothes, shop with a purpose. Consider dress codes for work and events you are likely to attend.

DRESS CODES

This is only a rough guide because your own personality must also shine through. Sometimes an invitation will state the dress code by saying:

Black tie – For men, this means a black (or white) tuxedo with a bowtie, and for ladies, it means a full-length evening dress with glitz and glamor.

Formal – Men should wear a dark suit with a formal tie. Ladies still wear an evening dress, but it can be less elaborate and shorter to mid-calf.

Semi-formal – A suit is required for men, but it does not have to be a dark color. You should still wear a tie. Ladies wear a dress with sleeves, preferably in a plain color and no shorter than knee length. Tailored trousers with a matching tailored jacket and smart blouse are also acceptable.

Business smart/ smart - This is similar to semi-formal but will vary from company to company depending on the industry. Creative companies will lean towards being more relaxed, and financial or legal companies will be more formal.

Business casual/smart casual - Wear something comfortable, but you should still look acceptable if you bump into a client. Fitted longer shorts or jeans with a golf shirt or open-neck shirt can be worn by men, while the ladies wear a knee-length skirt/fitted shorts and a blouse.

Casual – This usually means you can come 'as you are.' Although being comfortable is the main aim, you should still ensure that your clothes are clean. Avoid T-Shirts with slogans and ripped or ragged trousers unless you are hanging out with your fam.

Dress codes for specific events

Weddings - Afternoon and evening weddings usually require black tie or formal garments. Morning weddings are smart or business smart

Cocktail Party – Formal

Dinner party – Smart

Business or Company dinner - Business smart unless the invitation indicates 'formal' or black tie

An Interview - Business smart

Religious ceremonies - Smart but avoid open shoulders, clingy fabrics, plunging necklines, and open backs

Funerals - Smart in muted or dark colors

Theater, ballet, or opera - Smart casual

First date - Depends on the venue but usually casual and comfortable is best

Family get-togethers or barbeque - Casual and comfortable

BASIC SEWING SKILLS

Learning some basic sewing skills to keep your clothes in good repair is a smart thing to do. Sewing is not only for the ladies; even men in the military are expected to do repairs such as sew on buttons and re-stitch hems and seams. Invest in a small basic sewing kit with a small pair of scissors, needles, a few pins, and thread in various colors.

Threading a needle

- Using the scissors, snip the end of the thread at an angle to give a clean, sharp edge.
- Hold the needle up to the light and push the end of the thread through the hole.
- Double the thread for a length of at least 3 inches or completely for double thread stitching.
- Hold the end of the thread and wind it around your index finger three times.

- Roll the threads between your thumb and forefinger, and pull them tight to make a knot.

Stitching on a button

- Try to re-stitch buttons before they fall off.
- Choose a thread that matches the garment.
- Hold the button where it should be, ensuring it aligns with the other buttons and the buttonhole.
- Push the threaded needle up through the fabric from the wrong side of the garment and through one hole in the button until the knot is resting against the garment.
- Now insert the needle from the top (right side of the garment) down through the other hole in the button.
- Pull the thread all the way through on each stitch.
- Repeat this up and down, stitching between the holes in the button until the button is secure.
- Working on the wrong side of the garment, secure the thread at the back of the button with a few stitches.

Stitching a hem

- Using the pins, replace the hem where it should be.
- With a threaded needle in a matching color, pull the thread through the edge of the hem fabric with the knot trapped between the hem and the garment.

- Using the needle, gently lift a few strands of the garment just above the hem edge and pull the thread through.
- Insert the needle into the hem edge approximately 3 mm from the edge and pull the thread through. Do not pull too tightly.
- Repeat lifting a few strands of the garment about ½ inch further along and then catch the hem edge as before. Continue stitching between the garment and the hem edge until the hem is secured.
- On the wrong side of the garment, this produces diagonal stitches on the edge of the hem, and on the right side, it makes tiny, barely visible stitches.

Repairing a seam

- Working on the inside of the garment, hold the seam with the edges aligned and following the line of the original stitching, stitch with the threaded needle as follows.
- Insert the threaded needle from the back to the front a short distance into where the stitching is still holding. Pull the thread up until the knot is resting against the fabric.
- Insert the needle from the front to the back about 3 mm to the right along the stitching line, and pull the thread through to the back.

- Move the needle to about 6mm to the left of the stitch you have just made, and bring it up through the fabric to the front.
- Insert the needle 3mm to the right and through to the back, making the second stitch.
- Continue working small stitches along the seam line until you have closed the gap in the seam. Work a little further along into where the stitching is still good and secure the threads.

HOW TO IRON

Always check the garment label to get information on what temperature to use for ironing. See below for the laundry symbols. Sort the garments into groups according to the temperature needed and start with the lowest temperature. Use a low temperature to iron delicate fabrics and a medium to high temperature for linen, cotton, and denim.

Wherever possible, iron on the wrong side of the fabric or use a clean cloth over the garment to protect it. Steam will help speed up the process but is unsuitable for all materials. You can spray the garment slightly with water or use a damp cloth. Test the iron's temperature first on an inside seam or hem to ensure it is not too hot for the fabric.

Use a sturdy ironing board and work carefully with the iron – it will be hot, and you can burn yourself. Always keep the iron upright when resting on the ironing board, and only store it when it has cooled down completely.

Top Tip

To get wrinkle-free cotton and linen clothes, insert a strip of tinfoil (shiny side up) under the cover of your ironing board. This will help to heat from two directions, resulting in a more efficient ironing process.

Ironing a Shirt or Blouse

1. Start with the collar in the center of the underside. Work the iron along to the edge.
2. Turn and work to the other edge.
3. Drape the shoulder section over the ironing board's end and work the iron from the front to the back of the shoulder.
4. Repeat with the other shoulder.
5. Next, iron the cuff of one sleeve. Fold the sleeve in half with the fold line down the middle and iron both sides.
6. Repeat with the other sleeve.
7. Then drape the shirt or blouse over the ironing board with the collar towards the pointed end and the button/buttonhole edge aligned with the far side of the ironing board. Smooth the fabric to ensure that you only iron one layer at a time.

8. Iron the shirt's body, starting at the button/buttonhole edge of the right-hand side of the garment, working from collar to hem.
9. Continue all around the body of the garment, shifting it around on the board.
10. Work across the back and then the left-hand side up to the button/buttonhole edge.
11. Use the tip of the iron to work around the buttons.
12. Hang the shirt up immediately or fold it neatly.

Ironing Trousers or Pants

Before placing the trousers on the ironing board:

1. Pull out the pockets and iron them flat.
2. Drape the trousers over the pointed end of the ironing board and work from the waist down on the inside of the pants.
3. Iron the waistband and then work the iron all around the hip section, shifting the trousers as you go.
4. Where you can lift the pockets, iron under them, or if they are fixed, press lightly over them.
5. Next, lay one leg over the board with the seams aligned as best you can, and iron both sides of the trousers leg.
6. Work your way down to the hem and repeat with the other leg. Hang the trousers right side out with the

inner leg seams aligned and loosely folded over the hanger.

Ironing Skirts and Dresses

Work from the top down, following the same method for blouses to the waistline. Then drape the skirt over the ironing board with the waistline at the narrow part of the ironing board and work your way around the skirt, shifting the garment as you go.

Top Tip: Keep your iron in good condition

- *Empty any water left in the iron before storing it.*
- *Clean the iron surface regularly with a damp cloth or an iron cleaner.*

Laundry

Have you ever noticed that your laundry pile never seems to go away? One way to stay on top of it is by designating a day for laundry, like how they used to do it in the Victorian Era, with Monday being the traditional laundry day. Setting a specific day will help you to plan and schedule your time more effectively.

Did you know that according to scientists, 70% of the dirt on your clothes is not visible to the naked eye? Therefore, always keep your clothes fresh and launder them after wearing them, even if you think it is still clean. Tailored jackets and trousers must be professionally dry-cleaned every 3 – 6 months. You can wash shirts, blouses, skirts, and dresses following the instructions on the labels.

Always remove spots and stains with a stain remover. Spray on the mark and leave for a few minutes, then wash. A paste made from 2 tablespoons of bicarbonate soda and one tablespoon of water will also help remove stains. Apply the paste and allow it to dry, then brush or vacuum off. You can also use this paste to clean carpets and upholstery.

Top Tip

Clean the washing machine by occasionally running a full cycle with hot water and two cups of white vinegar. This will remove any bacteria and leave the machine sanitized. Finish by running a second cycle with water to ensure all the vinegar is rinsed.

Laundry symbols

Laundry symbols can be confusing, so here is a quick and easy way to read laundry instructions. There are six basic symbols:

Washing	Bleaching	Drying
Ironing	Tumble drying	Dry cleaning

All instructions are a variation of these symbols. Additional symbols mean the following:

Hand – perform an action by hand, not by machine

Crossed through – do not use this action

Dots – indicate temperatures, 1 dot = low, 2 dots = medium and 3 dots = hot, etc.

Numbers – specific temperatures are given.

Letters – Indicate to the dry cleaners which chemicals to use

Here is a complete guide with all the symbols:

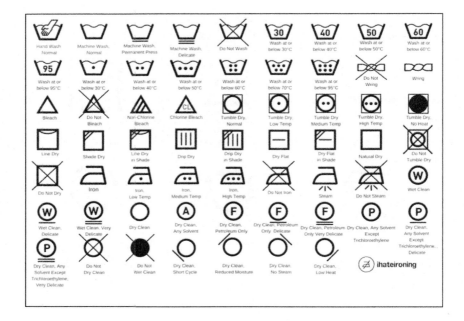

What detergent to use

The choice of detergent will depend on whether you wash the clothes in an automatic washing machine or by hand. Automatic washing machines need a detergent that will not create too many suds or lather excessively. Read the instructions on the detergent for information on what quantity to use.

Delicate fabrics such as silk, wool, and some evening wear are best washed by hand and dried flat. Use a detergent for hand washing.

To save time when doing your laundry:

1. Sort your clothes into three groups when placing them into the hamper – light colors or whites, bright colors, and dark colors.
2. Wash these groups separately to avoid colors running. You can also add a color catcher to the machine for extra color protection.
3. Place the clothes in the washing machine and select a wash cycle. The instruction manual will give you guidelines.
4. Never overfill the machine - the clothes should have room to tumble as they are washed.

Folding clothes

Fold clothes soon after washing and ironing to ensure that you are neatly dressed with minimum ironing. Neatly pack your clothes into the closet so you can always find items you want quickly.

Folding T-Shirts, shirts, and sweaters

1. Place the T-Shirt flat on a clean surface with the front down.
2. Fold the left sleeve and side towards the middle to halfway into the shoulder seam.
3. Fold down long sleeves, so the cuff is in line with the hem edge.

4. Repeat on the right-hand side. Now fold the hem edges up to the shoulders.

This basic fold works for all tops, golf shirts, shirts, blouses, etc. Close buttons before starting to fold. Straighten the collar as the last step in the process.

For hoodies, fold the hood down towards the waist before bringing the hem edge up to the shoulders.

Trousers

Fold the trousers in half with the inner seams aligned. Bring the hems up to the waist and then fold once more.

Towels and bed linen

1. Hold the towel lengthwise and bring the hem edges together to fold it in half.
2. Repeat this step, and then place the towel on a flat, clean surface in front of you.
3. Fold the left side to the center and then repeat with the right-hand side.
4. Fold the bottom edge to the top edge.

Use this same folding method for flat sheets repeating several times to make the folded sheet about the size of a pillowcase.

Fitted sheets:

1. Fold in half lengthwise and crosswise so that all the gathered corners are together.
2. Place on a clean flat surface and fold the top and sides in, with the corners overlapped.
3. Fold lengthwise and crosswise until the sheet is the size of a pillowcase.

PACKING A SUITCASE

When traveling, you always want to have minimal luggage as it gives you more freedom and flexibility during your trip. By packing only the essentials, you will have an easier time navigating through crowded areas at the airport, quickly collecting your baggage, making impromptu plans without worrying about your belongings, and spending less time keeping track of your gear.

Gather all the items that you think you will need. Eliminate some things you can do without for a few days. You will need three lower garments and four to five tops for a five-day trip. Select items in the same colorway so that you can mix and match. Also, choose garments that are versatile enough to dress up or down. My friend Anna always packs lightly. Instead of packing a cocktail dress, she packs a sparkly necklace to add to her daytime black trousers and black top. It saves her space, and she looks good during the day and sparkles at dinner at night. Where possible, select fabrics that don't crease easily. Fold everything up following the directions given previously in this chapter.

Place socks and small items such as chargers inside your shoes. Place shoes into plastic bags so that they don't soil your clothes. Always place heavy items like shoes and toiletry bags into the suitcase first, so they are at the bottom, and try to level out this layer. Make sure that all liquid containers are well closed. You can also place them in zip-lock bags to prevent leakage. Next, add the smaller clothing items, alternating collars, and folded edges. Lastly, place the longer items such as trousers and dresses using the full width and length of the suitcase.

Jewelry should be placed in a small container, and this, together with belts, scarves, and warm hats, can be placed around the edges of the suitcase or in the corners to fill little gaps. Lastly, pack a laundry or dry cleaning bag for dirty folded clothes when returning.

HYGIENE IS IMPORTANT

'Hygiene' is a term used in many situations, from personal to business management. It means looking after what you have to ensure no problems arise later. Here we are talking about personal hygiene. Keeping your body clean will help to prevent you from getting sick. Regular washing and bathing rid the body of germs before they can erode your immune system.

Dental care

Do you want sparkling white teeth and fresh breath? Brush your teeth at least twice a day. With a ½ inch squeeze of toothpaste and a brush, work along your upper and lower teeth brushing up and down to remove any food that is stuck. Remember to pay attention to the back of the teeth as well. Brushing should last for at least 2 minutes. Gently floss between your teeth to remove plaque that was missed by the brush bristles.

Body

A fresh-smelling body is possible if you use warm water and soap to shower or bath every day. Dry your skin well with an absorbent towel, and use a moisturizing lotion if your skin is dry. Always apply deodorant.

Hands

On average, our hands carry over 3000 germs at any time. So, wash your hands frequently, especially after you have been to the bathroom, in public places, and before eating. Avoid touching your face with unwashed hands. With warm water and soap, rub between the fingers and scrub the tips of the fingers and the palms for at least 20 seconds to remove germs. Pay attention to getting dirt out from under your fingernails. Use a nail brush if necessary.

Face

You can use a facial wash or crème cleanser to remove dirt particles. Pat your face dry and apply a moisturizer with sunscreen to keep your skin from getting dry and damaged. If you are battling to keep your face clear of pimples, use an over-the-counter solution or visit your local General Practitioner, who can prescribe something to help.

Facial hair

If you grow a mustache or beard, keep it clean by washing daily and trimming it evenly and neatly.

Shaving

Whether you are a guy shaving your face, or a girl shaving your legs and armpits, take care to avoid cutting yourself. Here are some tips:

- Wet your skin and hair to soften it. It's easiest to shave while showering or bathing when the skin is warm and pliable.
- Apply shaving cream or gel. If you have sensitive skin, use a product, especially for this purpose.
- Shave in the direction of the hair. Shaving in the opposite direction can damage the hair follicle and lead to rashes, razor bumps, razor burns, and nicks in the skin.
- Start at the top and work down in strips, slightly overlapping to cover the entire area.

- Rinse the razor blade frequently to prevent clogging and blunting the blade. Change the blade or use a new disposable razor after about five shaves. This will vary depending on how thick your hair is.
- Ensure you clean your razor after you shave and allow it to dry completely before storing it.

Hair

Wash your hair regularly to prevent it from becoming oily. Usually, teenagers need to wash their hair every day, but if your hair tends to be dry, you can wash it every second day. Choose a shampoo that is suitable for your hair type. The quantity of shampoo will depend on the length of your hair. Wet your hair, apply sufficient shampoo to create a good all-over lather, and gently massage your scalp with your fingertips. Wash long strands of hair to the tips as well. Rinse well and wrap a towel around your head to absorb excess water. Remember to work gently with wet hair, so you don't damage it. If you use a hairdryer, hold it at least 6 – 7 inches away from your scalp and set it to medium heat only.

Did you know?

63% of people enjoy singing while they shower. The privacy of the shower makes it a great place to practice high notes. Singing can be a form of therapy. So, the next time you're in the shower, sing your favorite tune and use the time to de-stress!

LADIES – THIS IS FOR YOU.

Having a period does not mean that you have to put your life on hold. It just means that you can take a little extra care of yourself. Find products that work with your lifestyle and give you the protection you need. Tampons and sanitary pads come in various sizes and absorbency to cater to all situations. Keep track of your cycle and ensure that you are prepared for the start of a period with your choice of tampon, sanitary pad, or menstrual cup. Shower or bathe at least once a day and wash your hair more frequently – keeping yourself fresh will make you feel much better.

No matter which product you choose to use, change it frequently, every 3 to 4 hours, regardless of whether your period is light or heavy. Bacteria build up very quickly and can cause an odor. After removing a tampon, wrap it up in toilet paper, place it in a disposable bag, seal and throw it away in the bin. Sanitary pads can be rolled from one side to the other along the length, with the soiled part inside the roll and the adhesive part outside. Then, dispose of it the same way you would for tampons. Many public places have bins for this purpose inside each stall, but most bathrooms have a dustbin near the basins. If you use a menstrual cup, you can check and change it less frequently. Once you have removed it, tip the liquid into the toilet. Since public bathrooms can be busy, having a spare one in your handbag is a good idea. Insert the clean menstrual cup, then go to the basin and wash out the used one with warm water and soap. Dry with a tissue or hand towel and replace it in your handbag as your spare one.

Help for those days

If you are experiencing pain or cramps, use a hot water bottle or heating pad to ease it. Various products are on the market – although you must plug some into a heating source. Still, if you are on the go or can't take time off work or lessons, there are others available at the pharmacy that are battery-operated or even chemical-based ones that emit heat as soon as they are opened.

A novelist and writer, Fyodor Dostoevsky, said, "If you want to be respected by others, the great thing is to respect yourself." Keeping yourself clean and well-groomed and wearing freshly laundered appropriate clothes shows that you respect yourself, and you will find that other people take you more seriously and view you as an adult. It is far easier to get into good habits now while you are still young than to correct bad habits later in life.

4

TAKE CONTROL OF YOURSELF
AND YOUR HOME

L aunching out on your own can be a roller coaster
of feelings. Partly exciting but partly terrifying.
Don't worry; take it step-by-step, starting with the
most urgent. We'll look at how to find somewhere to live,
manage that space, set some goals, and find the time to do all
this without losing control or getting overwhelmed. Does
this sound like a good plan? Then let's get started...

GETTING A ROOF OVER YOUR HEAD

You're dreaming of a top-floor penthouse with glowing
clean surfaces and all the devices that you need to make life
easy while you sip your favorite drink next to a sparkling
pool. It's good to dream, but this is real life. Let's just start

with where you are, and then work towards where you want to be.

- *Check your budget* –Rent must be paid every month and so this is probably the most important deciding factor on where you are going to live. You need to be able to afford the space you are renting, or you'll find yourself facing eviction. While you check your budget, don't forget to factor in the cost of utilities, transport, and possibly insurance.
- *Do some research* – Once you have decided on what you can afford, you can look at the area around your college or work. If you look further than a 5 km radius, transport will become expensive, so start with the areas that are closest. Eliminate the areas that are out of your price range and focus only on those areas that you can afford. Remember this is a starting point, not where you will be living for the rest of your life.
- *Contact agents* – Once you have decided where you can afford to live, you can contact agents for that particular area. Many have websites that list the housing they have on offer. Look through the lists using filters to exclude extras that you don't need. If you don't own a car, it's a waste to pay for the use of a garage or parking space.
- *Always view the property in person* – Photos can easily be retouched and manipulated, so always ask to view

the unit you are considering. Check for the following faults: Cracks or large patchy marks on the walls, ceilings, and carpets, may indicate a problem with dampness or a leaking hot water tank. A unit should have a window that can open for ventilation or it must have an air-conditioner. Open faucets/ taps to check that water is flowing and switch on the lights to check that there is a power source. Check the general security and cleanliness of the surrounding area as well.

- *Read through the lease/rental documents carefully* – Before signing any papers, make sure that you understand everything. The agreement should be clear about the deposit amount, the monthly rental, the occupation date, the date when rent is due, the length of the lease, and the length of the notice period.

Housing options for tight budgets

Stay at home

Whether you are working or studying, this is still a good option. It has the advantage of avoiding a major move, and you're also unlikely to have to do all the cooking and cleaning, although your help will be appreciated. Talk to your parents and negotiate the boundaries – they may be open to relaxing some of the rules if you are showing that you are more mature.

Make sure you get involved with what's happening on campus or at work and connect socially with other students or colleagues.

University residence

There are various criteria for applying, and if you qualify to live at the university, this can give you the best of two worlds. You'll have greater independence and freedom but still, have your meals cooked. Cleaning and laundry will be your responsibility, though. It is much easier to get involved in social activities and sports if you live on campus.

Private Accommodation

If you don't qualify for student housing or choose to live in private accommodation, you'll have complete freedom and independence and all the responsibility of cooking, cleaning, laundry, etc. Remember, factor in all the living costs of food, transport, and utilities when calculating your budget.

Co-renting

With this option, costs are halved, but make sure you set up with someone you get along well. Sharing with a total stranger can be anything from awkward to difficult. Sometimes it's best to live at home or alone for the first year, and then once you have made friends, you can switch to this option from the second year. Communicate with your flatmate to share the chores and responsibilities and ensure you do your share.

PAYING YOUR BILLS

In a previous chapter, we talked about building your credit score. One way to do just that is to pay your bills on time.

- Make a list of all your bills. The budget template that you drew up will help.
- Find out when the payments are due and use a calendar app to set reminders. Act on those reminders immediately after you get the alert.
- Try to pay the total monthly amount that is due. If you fall behind on payments, it will become challenging to catch up, and your credit score will be negatively affected. Minimum monthly payments indicate the minimum amount you **have** to pay if you have revolving credit. You should pay at least this amount, but if you can, pay a little more to keep interest amounts low.
- You can set up amounts that are the same each month to pay automatically on a specific day of the month.
- It is a good idea to pay your bills the day after you get paid. This way, you can forget about bills until next month, but you'll have a realistic balance of what is left in your bank account.

WHAT TO DO WHEN THINGS GO WRONG?

After a busy day of moving, you've been relaxing for about 20 minutes, and you hear water dripping. After another 5 minutes, you realize that the drips are falling more quickly. It dawns on you that this is your home and your problem. As you walk through the kitchen, you notice a huge puddle of water forming on the kitchen floor. It seems to be coming from the cupboard under the sink. Sure enough, at the bottom of that U-shaped pipe, there is water dripping. What should you do? First, find the shutoff point for the water supply and shut it off. Then find someone who can fix it.

Calling in help to sort out problems is best done quickly because minor issues can escalate quickly and become emergencies. Research the following service providers for your area. Ask for recommendations, compare general pricing, then save the contact details of two or three service providers:

A **plumber** will help with water-related problems for basins, baths, faucets/taps, toilets, drains, and leaks, such as in the above example.

An **electrician** will help with lighting, wiring, electric cords, and power issues.

You can call a **pest control specialist** to get rid of pests such as ants, termites, cockroaches, rats and mice, and small animals.

A **handyman** can help fix cupboards, closets, tiles, floors, doors, air conditioners, and glass in windows.

Mechanics know how to get your car running again and service it regularly.

A **Locksmith** will help with locks that are difficult to open or if you have lost your keys, are locked out of the house, or need keys cut.

CLEANING AND MANAGING YOUR HOME

One of the biggest shocks of setting up a home is that everything is now your responsibility, and it can feel overwhelming. Soon you'll settle into a routine and have it all under control. Not everything needs to be done every day. You can spread the cleaning out over a week. Use your favorite calendar app and set up a schedule following this suggestion, or adapt this schedule to what suits you:

Every day – Tidy up surfaces, make your bed, wash dishes, and clear garbage.

Monday – Declutter, dust, and remove cobwebs; thoroughly clean the living area.

Tuesday - Sweep or vacuum and mop the floors.

Wednesday – Thoroughly clean the basin, bath, shower, and toilet.

Thursday – Clean the kitchen well, wiping cupboards and appliances and clearing out uneaten food from the refrigerator.

Friday – Thoroughly clean the bedroom and study.

Saturday – Tackle the laundry and ironing.

Sunday – Have a rest or catch up on tasks missed during the week.

Why should you clean? After all, it's your space, and you don't mind if it's messy. Keeping your environment in order will give you a sense of achievement and prevent embarrassment if your fam comes over to hang out. But the most important reason is to eliminate pests, germs, and allergens, which can spread disease and seriously affect your health.

Before you rush out and buy a whole lot of expensive cleaning materials, know that many cheap household ingredients do a superb job of cleaning. Baking soda, vinegar, lemon juice, and salt are just a few that you can use. Warm water and a few drops of general-purpose cleaner or dishwashing liquid with added energy will also go a long way to keeping things clean. So, here are some tips on how to get the cleaning done quickly and easily:

Dusting

Before you start, tidy up the counter surfaces by putting away anything that shouldn't be there. It is best to have a specific place for everything and keep things in that place.

Flicking a duster around does not help much – you'll stir up the dust, and then when you turn around and walk out of the room, it'll settle again. You'll want to wipe the dust away using a slightly damp cloth with a bit of texture. A washcloth kept only for dusting or an old towel cut into smaller pieces will be ideal. The texture gives a gentle scrub as you wipe and helps to lift dirt. Wash the cloth out regularly while you are working so you are constantly wiping with a clean cloth. Work your way over the top of furniture, along shelves, picture frames, display items, TV screens, monitors, etc.

Vacuuming

Before vacuuming, move items from the floor where possible. Working under chairs and around chair legs will not be as successful as it would be if you moved the chair and vacuumed the entire surface of the carpet or floor. Use the attachment for carpets and switch over to the floor rubber attachment. Many vacuum cleaners also have a narrow attachment for corners and edges and an upholstery attachment for couches and soft chairs. Work in parallel strips until you have cleaned the entire room. Empty or replace the vacuum bag regularly and keep the attachments clean.

Mopping floors

Do you want to cut down on cleaning? Then, mop floors immediately after sweeping or vacuuming to get the most effective result. Half fill a bucket with warm water and add a few drops of detergent such as floor cleaner or dishwashing liquid. Allow the mop to soak in the water for 5 – 10 minutes to ensure it is thoroughly wet. Then squeeze out the excess water well. Starting at the far corner of the room, opposite the door. Move the mop backward and forward and side to side over small areas at a time, rinsing the mop thoroughly before moving to the next small area. Repeat until the entire floor is clean.

Getting rid of cobwebs

Cobwebs can gather in the most out-of-the-way places, so check the top corners of shelves, corners of rooms, under furniture, and skirtings. Use a feather duster with a long handle to deal with high-up cobwebs or ones in out-of-the-way places. Move the feather duster backward and forward or side to side to displace them.

Keeping bathrooms clean

Mirrors – A few sprays of commercial window cleaner wiped off with a paper towel will keep your glass and mirror surfaces sparkling.

Basins and bath – Remove any build-up of hair in the plug hole. Then with a damp cloth and general-purpose cleaner, wipe out the basin, paying special attention to the area around the drain. Wipe the faucets/taps and the outside of the basin too.

Toilet – Use a toilet brush to scrub out the bowl with an antibacterial cleaner. You can also use this mixture to deodorize the bathroom: Mix 1 cup of baking soda with 15 drops of tea tree essential oil and 15 drops of lemon or orange essential oil. Leave the mixture in the toilet bowl for 30 minutes and scrub again before flushing.

Cleaning the kitchen

With constant preparation of raw foods, especially chicken, fish, and eggs, it is necessary to wipe down the counters with a sanitizer or antibacterial cleaner. Remember to regularly wipe down the cupboard doors, handles of doors and drawers, sink, and appliances. Deal with spills immediately when they occur when it is easy to wipe up.

Dealing with garbage

Do you want a home that smells fresh all the time? You can reduce the need for expensive air fresheners and diffuses by simply controlling the items that cause odors. The biggest offender here is the garbage. Remove all garbage to an outside bin once a day. Find out which day of the week garbage is collected and take it to the curb where it can be picked up.

Eliminate clutter

You'll be amazed at how much clutter builds up in a home. Plan a decluttering day regularly and deal with the things that are building up:

- Collect advertising brochures, save the contact details, and recycle them.
- Starting in the living room with a laundry basket, pick up any items that are out of place. Move to the kitchen, check the basket for things that should be in the kitchen, and replace them. Look for items that are out of place in the kitchen and place them in the laundry basket. Move to the study and repeat the process. Eventually, you will return to the living room to replace items you collected elsewhere, and everything will be back where it should be.
- Remember to place the recycling bins out on collection day. If your town or city does not offer this service, take the recycling to the nearest depot weekly or bi-weekly.

Washing dishes

Yes, there is a correct way to do dishes. Well, there are several ways, but here is the most efficient:

- Wash out the sink bowl using a damp cloth and a few drops of dishwashing liquid.
- Half-fill the basin with hot water and a small amount of dishwashing liquid so that suds form. (The water should only be as hot as your hands can stand).
- If you have a second basin, half-fill with clear warm water to rinse dishes. Or, you can use a large bowl placed next to the sink.

- Start by washing glassware. You want to use the cleanest water to get your drinking glasses sparkling clean. A bottle brush will easily get to the base of the inside. Wipe the lip carefully to remove residue.
- Next, wash the knives, forks, and spoons. Fold the washcloth over, with the eating part of the utensil sandwiched in the middle, and wipe thoroughly.
- Next, wash cups by pushing the cloth to the bottom and twisting it around. Wipe the rim well.
- Wash saucers, side plates, and dinner plates by wiping the cloth over the surface a few times. Remember also to wash the back of the crockery.
- Finally, wash out pots or items that were very dirty, getting into the corners well.
- Change the water any time you think it is getting too dirty. You may use two or three sinks of fresh water if there are many dishes.
- Dry off the dishes with a soft, absorbent dish towel and pack them away.

Top Tip

Making a stainless steel pot or pan shiny again is easy. After you have cleaned it with warm water and soap:

1. *Rewash it using vinegar.*
2. *Mix a 1/2 cup of vinegar with 1 ½ cups of water to remove a build-up of white calcium deposits.*
3. *Pour into the pot and bring the mixture to a boil.*

Allow the mixture to cool, and then wash the pot with warm water and soap.

STAYING ORGANIZED

There are many ways of staying organized, but one Japanese method is called Kaizen, meaning 'good change,' and introduces five positive ways to get organized.

Sort (Seiri) –Anything unnecessary is distracting and should be eliminated.

Set in order (Seition) – Assign a place to keep each item and then keep it in its place.

Shine (Seiso) –A clean environment is organized and safer and shows that you respect yourself.

Standardize *(Seiketsu)* – Make your own rules (such as a schedule) and follow them.

Sustain (Shitsuke) – Continually improve systems and adopt the improved way of doing things.

Following this plan will ensure you have a clean, organized home and won't waste time trying to find things. That sounds like a great idea! Here are some more ideas:

- Get rid of old tech – if the phone is broken and you have a new one, take it to a recycling place. If it still works, then donate it to a charity.

- Neaten electric wires by rolling them to the needed length and securing them with a cable tie.
- Keep recycling items in a neat place.
- Donate items that you never use.
- Organize small items inside drawers into stackable boxes or containers.
- Keep keys on a rack in a handy place where you can find them when you need them.
- Deal with paperwork immediately by scanning and saving digitally or punching holes in the paper and placing them in a file.

MANAGING YOUR TIME

Would you like to have endless free time to do the things that you love to do? Yes? Then take control of your time and manage it effectively. Here's how to create a daily schedule and develop a routine.

1. Start with a downloadable planner for 1 – 3 months

Many planners are available, so look for one that allows you to add and delete items when needed.

2. Transfer the most important information to your planner

These will be the events you cannot miss without serious consequences- such as assignment deadlines for college, booked appointments, work shifts, important family events, etc.

3. Enter other important items

Next, add the things you must do but may be more flexible, like upcoming assignments, weekly sports participation, and studying for tests.

4. Fill in the items that you need to do but are not time sensitive

Grocery shopping, cleaning, laundry, or catching up on yard work will fit into this category.

5. Now, fill in the items you would like to have time to do.

Life needs balance, so you must plan to play baseball or watch that TV series to avoid getting too busy to do it. Fit these in where there may be a gap in the schedule or when deadlines are not urgent.

6. Add times to your weekly planner

Add specific times to the items on your weekly list and shuffle them into chronological order. Remember to allow time for commuting.

7. Color code everything

You can pick the colors, but I use Red (1) for the 'must do/ urgent' tasks, Orange (2) for the 'other important events,' Blue (3) for routine tasks, and Green (4) for the fun stuff. You can do it as a chart or as a list- whatever suits you best.

My planner for this week looks like this:

Monday - (3) Cleaning 7 am -8.30 am; (1) Work shift 9 am to 2 pm; (3) Buy groceries 2 pm – 3 pm; (1) Finish chemistry assignment 4 pm to 6 pm; (3) Supper 6.30 pm; (2) Study for Wednesday's test 7 pm to 9 pm; (4) Watch series on telly 9 pm to 10 pm

Tuesday: (3) Drop off recycling 7.30 am; (1) Submit Chemistry assignment 9 am; (1) Attend Chemistry lecture from 9 am to 10.30 am; (4) Hang out with friends until 12 pm; (3) Cleaning (Tues & Wed) 12.30 pm -2 pm; (1) Study for tomorrow's test 2.30 pm – 6 pm; (3) Supper 6.30 pm; (2) Homework for statistics lecture until 9.30 pm

Wednesday: (1) Revise math formulae 7.30 am to 8.30 am; (1) Math test 9 am to 11 am; (1) Work double shift 11.30 am - 6 pm; (3) Supper 6.30 pm; (2) Start English assignment 7 pm -9 pm; (4) Bedtime 10 pm

Thursday: (3) Cleaning 7 am-8 am; (1) Attend Chemistry lecture 9 am – 10.30 am; (1) Attend Statistics lecture 10.30 am – 12 pm; (4) Pizza with Mike; (1) Work shift 2.30 pm – 5.30 pm; (3) Supper 6 pm; (2) Work on English assignment; (3) Bedtime 10 pm

Friday: (3) Cleaning 7 am -8.30 am; (1) Botony prac/lecture 9 am-12 pm; (1) Chemistry prac 1 pm -4 pm; (1) Hand in English Assignment 4 pm; (1) Work shift 5 pm to 10 pm

Saturday: (3) Laundry and declutter day 9 am-1 pm; (3) Cook and freeze meals; (4) Baseball game at the park 2 pm – 6 pm; (1) Work shift 6.30 pm – 10.30 pm

Sunday: (4) Chill out; (2) Lunch with mom and dad 11.30 am to 2 pm; (1) Work shift 2.30 – 5.30; (4) Supper 6 pm; (3) Catch up on tasks: Ironing; (3) Grocery list, Check week's schedule.

Notes:

- On Tuesday, I cleaned longer, doing Tuesdays and Wednesdays chores because I knew I had a double shift at work and would be too tired to clean on Wednesday. Working ahead is a really smart way to plan.
- Knowing I would be tired on Wednesday after a double shift, I gave myself an hour in the evening to do whatever I felt like before bedtime. I chose to use this time to catch up on social media.
- I scheduled at least three-weekend fun events – watching the telly, a baseball game, and chilling out on Sunday. A routine creates a good balance and allows me to find time to do fun things and connect with friends.
- Because Friday was a hectic day, I planned to sleep longer on Saturday morning and spend time at home, but I still used the time to get chores done at a slower pace.

- I used the downtime to connect with friends, meeting over lunch for a pizza or between lectures.
- On Saturday morning, I cooked some meals to freeze for the coming week because I will be very busy with assignments due and tests to study for. I fitted this in-between doing loads of laundry.

Developing a routine

Does having a set routine sound boring? It creates a structure that promotes mental, physical, and emotional health. Psychologists warn that an absence of a routine can lead to stress and feeling overwhelmed. So, before you make up your mind about it being boring, let's look at some benefits of having a routine.

- It makes you more efficient. I found that getting into the routine of cleaning every day and following my weekly schedule meant I got everything done and didn't have to think too hard about what to do next.
- It saves time. By the time the weekend came around, I could take some time to relax because the cleaning was up to date from having stuck to the routine.
- It gives a sense of achievement. Ticking tasks off the schedule will give you a sense of having accomplished something.
- It helps you to remember - I know that on a Monday after my work shift, I must buy groceries for the week. If I don't stick to this routine, I won't have the

ingredients to cook supper on Wednesday, and dashing to the shops several times a week to buy single items wastes time.

- It prevents procrastination - doing something at a specific time on a particular day becomes a habit, and you are less likely to put it off.
- It uses time efficiently - by scheduling cleaning every morning for an hour before heading out, my time is used wisely. A lot can be done in a short space of time if you focus on the task at hand.

SETTING GOALS

Think about this quote by Benjamin Franklin, *"by failing to prepare, you are preparing to fail."* Do you think that this could be true?

Imagine the secretary of defense sending troops into a war without a plan or a goal. Or, an archer just aimlessly shooting arrows instead of having a bullseye to aim at. What would the results be? Maybe this sounds dramatic, but in order to succeed, you must have a goal to strive towards.

So, ask yourself, what do I want to achieve in the next five years (or 12 months)? Let's see how Mike is doing with his goal to 'become a wetland researcher.' (You can fill in your own goal)

This is how he has approached his aim to achieve his goal. He set himself some SMART goals:

Specific – Mike (who) wants to get an ASC - Environmental Science degree (what) from the University of Washington Seattle (where) by 2026 (when) so that he can become a Wetland Impact Assessment Researcher (why).

Measurable – Mike has set the following milestones so that he can track each step in his plan. If necessary, he will redirect himself along the way to get back on track: Final school year – achieve a 2,5 GPA to apply; Semester 1 & 2 – pass every subject; Semester 3 & 4 – gain a 60% average; Semester 5 & 6 – Achieve a first-class pass.

Achievable - Mike has set himself a goal to attend extra math lessons twice per week this year to get the required score to apply. He aims to increase his test grades by 10 points. He will apply for a part-time job to get extra funding. He was honest with himself about what he can achieve.

Realistic – After much thought, Mike decided to cut back on baseball over weekends to work on math to increase his score.

Time-based - GPA score must be sufficient to apply by May 2023; Application to college due in June 2023; Pass the first year in 2024, Pass the second year in 2025; Pass the third year in 2026.

This is an example; you can complete your own set of SMART goals.

Okay, let's start at the beginning:

Figure out what you want – This may take some time, but the best way to do this is to take note of what catches your attention. Mike realized in his second last year of school that he was constantly watching documentaries on wetlands and was fascinated by climate change's impact on these areas.

Do some research – When Mike realized this was his interest, he began researching jobs that might be available in the future. He then found out that he would need a University degree. He would also need funding and increase his GPA scores to apply.

Figure out if your goal is realistic – He went to talk to his teacher, who was realistic about how his scores were not reasonably sufficient but encouraged him to work harder. He also spoke to his parents about funding. They said they could help, but he would also need a part-time job to contribute.

Focus on a plan – Mike had some doubts, but after some thought and talking with people he trusts, he realized that if he made some adjustments, he could achieve his goal. He cut his social media time to 15 minutes a day and began to work on his schoolwork to increase his scores. He also cut baseball practice to once a week to focus on his more important goal.

Keep yourself motivated - Goals are not always easy to achieve. Sometimes you have to sacrifice or take a longer route to get there. Mike is fortunate; not everyone has access to funding from their parents. You may have to work full-time after leaving school to earn money to fund your studies, or you may need to apply for a student loan and work part-time. Never give up on a goal that you really want!

It's okay if you haven't yet figured everything out for your future. Start with a tiny step by taking control of your immediate environment.

Admiral Navy Seal William McRaven got his audience laughing when he started his keynote address to college students by saying,

> *"If you want to change the world, start by making your bed. If you make your bed every morning, you will have accomplished the day's first task. It will give you a small sense of pride and encourage you to do another task and another, and by the end of the day, that one task completed will have turned into many completed tasks. Making your bed will also reinforce that the little things in life matter. If you can't do the little things right, you'll never be able to do the big things right. And, if by chance you have a miserable day, you'll come home to a bed that is made. That you made, and the made bed will encourage you that tomorrow will be better".*

The rest of his talk is available on the internet and worth listening to. Still, for now, the point is if you make one intentional decision to accomplish something, no matter how small, and follow through with it, you will be able to take control of another small area of your life. Before you know it, your life will have a purpose, and you will be able to stick to routines and focus on setting SMART goals to achieve what you want to.

5

TRAVEL SAFELY

Although our world looks very different since the pandemic, with many people opting to study and work online, travel is still part of our lives. The average American travels for about 55 minutes per day, and the average Briton for 63 minutes per day. This works out to almost one entire month per year and takes up about 20% of earnings.

Clearly, commuting is an integral part of our lives, so we will look at some basic navigational skills and safety tips for traveling.

NAVIGATING YOUR ROUTE

Consider learning basic navigation skills; you never know when you may need them. Electronics can sometimes fail, so don't rely solely on mobile apps, maps, and internet connectivity.

Reading maps

You can get a map from most gas/petrol stations or bookstores.

Choose the right kind of map:

To navigate through a city or town, you will need a map showing roads, road names, city freeways, and various buildings of interest.

For out-of-town navigation, you will need a map showing interstate highways, tourist sites, and the area's topography indicating rivers, lakes, mountains, and even hiking trails.

Check the orientation of the map:

All maps should have a compass icon showing North (N), South (S), West (W), and East (E). If you do not find this icon, you can assume that the top of the map is North.

Read the legend:

On one side of the map, there will be a 'key' or 'legend.' This explains what the various symbols on the map indicate. For example, all main roads may be displayed as a thick black line, and rivers may be marked as a blue line with pools of blue color showing lakes. Railway tracks may be shown as black lines with small lines at right angles across them. Forests may be shown as green triangles, and so on.

Check the scale of the map:

The map's scale is the ratio of the distance on the map to the distance on the ground and may differ from map to map. A map with a scale of 1: 500,000 means that one inch (2,5 cm) on the map represents 8 miles (12,87km) on the ground.

Using the map to get where you want to be:

- Figure out where you are on the map by looking for marked road names or features.
- Once you have established where you are, you can find the point where you want to be and then plot your route.
- It is a good idea to have a compass if you are traveling. Most mobile phones have one with the "tools" settings, or you can download an app. Remember to follow the instructions to calibrate it before leaving home.
- Align the North of the map with the North on the compass.
- Calculate the rough distance between landmarks by using the scale on the map.
- Make a note of features or buildings to look for as you travel. Road names, sites of interest, clumps of trees, and a river bend can all serve as checkpoints along the route.

North, South, East, West

How do you know which direction is where? The easiest way to tell is by the position of the sun. The sun rises in the East and sets in the West. If you imagine a circle around where you are standing, if East is where your right hand is pointing and West is opposite where your left hand is pointing, then North is the halfway point in front of you, and South is the halfway point behind you.

Another way to tell is with a compass. Place the compass on a flat surface, and the red arrow will point North. The other cardinal points of direction work in a clockwise direction East, South, and West.

READING TIMETABLES FOR PUBLIC TRANSPORT

Standing in front of the information board at the train or bus station can be daunting. But here is a little secret: All timetables have certain common features, and once you get to grips with these, you'll be on the move.

Timetables are given in a grid with columns and rows, each with its own heading. Find the column or row labeled with the name or number of the bus route you need to take, and then trace along the column/row that lists the stop at which you are standing. This will give you a block with a specific time, when the bus should arrive and when you should be ready to get onto the bus. Let's try that on the timetable below:

Location	Bus route 23 (Red)		Bus route 34 (Green)	
	Morning am	Afternoon pm	Morning am	Afternoon pm
Copthorne Corner	8.30	1.05	12.30	4.45
Crown Prince Hotel	8.45	1.20	12.45	5.00
Leisure Beach	8.50	1.25		
City Center	9.10	1.45		
Holiday Inn	9.20	1.55	1.10	1.15

You live one block away from Copthorne Corner and want to travel to the City Center, a five-minute walk from the mall, where you work a morning shift.

Looking at the blank grayed-out blocks makes it clear that you cannot take Bus 34 (Green route) because it does not go into the City Center. So, you must take Bus 23 or the red route. This bus leaves Copthorne Corner at 8.30, so you will need to leave home at 8.20 to get to Copthorne Corner in time to catch Bus 23 (Red Route). The timetable also tells you that the bus should arrive in the City Center at 9.10. Your shift starts at 9.30, so you will have plenty of time to walk to work from the City Center.

This is a very simplified timetable, but all transport timetables work similarly by giving times when they should arrive at a specific location. They may also provide a linear diagram with each route marked in a color. If there is no direct route, you can take a combination of routes to get to where you want to go.

TRAFFIC SIGNS AND TERMS

Every industry has its own jargon and terms, and it's important to know the meaning of some more common or important traffic terms so that when you listen to a radio traffic advisory or get directions, you understand. Have a look at these terms before commuting or traveling:

Back road – a secondary road through a rural area, maybe gravel.

Bicycle lane - space reserved for pedaled bicycles only. Cars and motorbikes may not use these lanes.

Boom barrier/gate – a pole across the road that restricts access.

Bottleneck – a build-up of slower traffic often due to several lanes converging as the road narrows.

Box junction – yellow criss cross markings on the road in the middle of an intersection. This area must be left open to prevent gridlocks in traffic.

Bus lane – reserved for buses only. Cars, motorbikes, and bicycles may not travel in these lanes.

Bus Rapid Transit (BRT) or Train Rapid Transit (TRT) – a system for commuting and carrying large numbers of people.

Bypass – mainline road that routes traffic around a city or high-traffic area.

Cats' eyes – the reflective markers that appear along the white line in the middle of the road. These are usually used in areas where there is heavy fog.

Congestion – high volume of traffic that can only move slowly.

Congestion fee/toll – some crowded cities charge a fee to drive through the center during peak hours.

Country lane – small, narrow road no wider than the width of one car. Find a spot to pull over so that the vehicle coming head-on can pass.

A crossing guard - sometimes called a lollipop man or woman who has the authority to temporarily stop traffic so that pedestrians can cross—is often seen outside schools or communal homes where the aged or disabled live.

Crossroads - two roads cross each other, and at that point, you are obliged to check carefully before crossing the path of traffic. In the US and some other countries, these may be controlled with 4-way stop signs, but this is different in the UK. The driver that arrives first at the intersection typically has the right of way. Watch carefully to ensure the road is clear before crossing or turning into the road.

Crosswalk/ Zebra Crossing – shown by straight, broad white stripes across the road, indicating a place for pedestrians to cross.

Cul-de-sac – a dead-end road that has no thoroughfare.

Detour – alternate route to avoid construction or road maintenance.

Floodway – an area of a road that floods easily during the rainy season.

Footpath or footway – an area reserved for pedestrians only – no cars or motorized vehicles are allowed.

Freeway or highway – roads outside of city centers, where you can travel at a higher but limited speed.

Gantry – overhead support for toll points.

Gridlock – traffic is so congested that it cannot move.

Growlers or rumble strips – vibration ridges to indicate that you must return to your side of the road.

Hairpin bend – a very sharp curve in the road that doubles traffic back in the opposite direction.

Highway patrol - police tasked with enforcing the law, especially on the roads.

LIFE SKILLS FOR TEENS | 123

Interchange – the point where several freeway roads come together and then diverge.

Intersection/ junction – where two or more roads cross over each other.

Kerb/curb – the raised edge between the road and pavement.

Level crossing - point where a road and a railway line cross over each other. Always stop and check for trains, and do not cross if the barrier is down. Trains have the right of way.

Merge – the point at which lanes are reduced in number because the road narrows.

One-way street – travel only in the direction indicated by the arrows.

Overpass – a road on a bridge that crosses over another road.

Overtake – to go around another vehicle to get in front.

Peak hour/ rush hour – usually occurs early morning or late afternoon when most people are traveling to or from work.

Pedestrian – a person walking alongside a road or crossing a road.

Right of way – the priority given to certain lanes of traffic.

Roundabout – several roads feed into a circular road.

Route marker – a numbered identifier that corresponds to the map.

Speed limit – the maximum speed that you can travel on that road.

Tail-gating - the act of following another car too closely.

Tollgate/barrier – a point at which tolls (a fee) are collected for using the road.

Underpass - the road that goes under a bridge.

U-turn - a 180° turn to continue in the direction from which you came.

Yield – stop or slow to give right of way to other traffic.

SAFETY WHEN TRAVELING

Traveling alone

Traveling alone is sometimes unavoidable but carries some risk. To keep yourself safe, you can minimize this:

- Research the route that you will need to travel. Online information can give you the actual street view so that you are familiar with landmarks at your destination.
- Allow friends and family information about your daily commute, especially if you work late shifts or need to walk after dark.
- Also, let friends or family know if your usual routine will change or if you are going out of town or using a

different route.

- If you are traveling out of town, let someone know where you are going and give them a rough estimate of when you will be back.
- Always be alert and aware of your surroundings.
- Keep to well-lit areas and walk or drive with a purpose rather than amble along.
- Be aware of travel scams or typical modus operandi of thieves in your area.
- Keep emergency contact details on your phone and write them down on paper to keep in your purse or wallet in case your phone doesn't work. This should include a contact person, local police, medical assistance, and insurance.
- Check weather reports before setting out, and be prepared for heavy rain, snow, and winds.
- Keep your valuables locked in the boot rather than on the seat.
- If you are walking or using public transport, place valuables in a sturdy bag that fits tightly to your body and cannot be snatched.
- Carry emergency cash in a well-hidden place.
- Stay sober!
- Avoid unnecessary risks – if you work until late at night and there are no people around, take a taxi from door to door.
- Learn basic self-defense techniques and carry pepper spray.

- Listen to your intuition - if something seems wrong, it likely is.

Breakdowns and emergencies

Do you want to avoid having a breakdown or emergency? Then, keep your car well-maintained with regular checks. Ensure you have basic tools in your boot, such as a wheel spanner, jack, and jumper leads. It is also a good idea to keep a flashlight, kneeling pad, and rain poncho in case you need them. Regularly check the pressure in the spare tire. Make sure that you have enough gas/petrol for the journey. Even so, you may have a problem, so here are guidelines on what to do:

Flat tire

If a tire is flat, your steering wheel will feel 'heavy.' Find a safe, well-lit place to pull well off the road. The ground should be level and away from a bend in the road. Engage the hand brake and switch on the hazard lights. Switch off the car. Display the warning triangle so that upcoming traffic can avoid you. Collect all the tools you need from the car's boot: a flashlight, jack, wheel spanner, kneeling pad, and rain poncho if necessary.

Loosen the lug nuts with the wheel spanner while the car is still on the ground. Insert the jack and crank the car high enough for the spare tire to clear the ground. Remove the lug nuts and lift the tire off. Place the spare tire in position and hand-tighten the lug nuts. Lower the car and then tighten the lug nuts with the wheel spanner. Replace all the tools in the boot, including your emergency triangle. Check that it is safe to re-enter the road while your hazard lights are still flashing. Once you are back up to speed, switch off the hazard lights.

Flat battery

If the battery is flat, the car won't start. You will need jumper leads and another vehicle with a charged battery.

Check which side of each car the battery is situated on, then park the cars with their noses towards each other with the shortest possible distance between the batteries without the cars touching. Ensure the hand brakes are engaged and both cars are switched off. Attach one end of the black jumper lead to the working battery's negative terminal (-) and the other end of the black lead to the flat battery's negative (-) terminal. Now attach one end of the red jumper lead to the working battery's positive terminal (+) and the other end of the red lead to the flat battery's positive terminal (+). Switch on the working car and allow it to run for about two minutes, then switch on the flat car. Allow both vehicles to run like this for about ten minutes.

Disconnect the leads in the reverse order and switch off the helper car. Leave the engine of the problem car running for as long as you can, or drive the car for a distance to charge the battery.

Get the problem battery checked at a battery center as soon as possible and replace it if necessary. Avoid leaving your car lights or fan running while parked, as this drains the battery.

Wise ways

- Never give strangers a lift, ever.
- Avoid traveling alone at night, or have someone meet you at your destination.
- Keep car doors locked when driving.
- Travel only on main roads unless absolutely unavoidable.
- Park in well-lit areas only.
- Leave at least a car length distance between you and the car in front. If sudden braking is necessary, you will also have time to stop without going into the vehicle in front.
- Reduce your speed when it rains, or there is fog, and increase the distance between you and the car in front.
- If your car is old, unreliable, or you are traveling far away, sign up for an app that allows a friend or family member to track you. If you do break down, help can get to you quickly.

OWNING A CAR

Although many cities and towns have good public transport systems, there may be a good reason to have your own vehicle.

Pros of having your own transport

- Train and bus routes are set and may not serve the route or times you must travel.
- You may work or live outside of the area serviced by the public transport system.

Cons of having your own vehicle

- Cars cost money – initial costs, maintenance costs, gas/petrol costs, insurance, and repair costs all mount up.

Buying a car

Having weighed up all these points, you may still want or need to buy a car.

Start with research

There are many options, from buying a brand-new car to purchasing a second-hand car or leasing a car on a short-term basis.

New car: This is the most expensive option, and you will need to put down a deposit and arrange a loan for the balance. Loans can be obtained through a bank or a car financing company, and interest will be added to the loan amount. You will also need to take out insurance as the bank wants to ensure they get their money. A new car is likely to be the most reliable.

Second-hand car: Only buy from a reputable dealer. You may still need to pay a deposit and arrange a loan, but the total amount spent will be less. Look for a car with a complete maintenance and service history and low mileage. This should be less than 10,000 miles (16 000 km) per year. So if the car is two years old, the mileage should be at most 20 000 miles (32 000 km). Buy a car less than five years old if you can afford it.

Rent a car: This is a good option if you can commute daily but need a car to travel further occasionally. You will need a valid driver's license and credit card.

Some companies have 'rent to own' options. You don't need a deposit, and although you initially rent the car, you can buy it when you can. Apart from not needing a deposit, the main benefit of this option is that you are the only driver, and you know that the car is in excellent condition when you decide to buy it.

Check your budget

Did you ever hear the joke about the guy whose dad gave him money to pay the utility bill, but instead, he used it to put down a deposit on a second-hand car? A few days later, a brand-new car arrived. The car belonged to the electrician who came to cut off the power.

Hee hee, jokes aside! Your decision on whether to buy a new car, a second-hand car, or rent a car will depend on what you can afford. Don't be tempted to reduce your budget on other necessities to buy a car. Remember to calculate the estimated cost of gas/petrol and insurance when choosing a car.

Finding the right car for you

Many online sites offer cars. You can set the filters for price range, age, car capacity, make, and model of the car you want. Work only with reputable websites and read reviews beforehand.

Never buy a car *only* online. Once you have selected two or three options, arrange to test drive them so that you can see what the car is like:

- Check the condition of the outside of the car.
- Open the hood to check the engine.
- Make sure it is reasonably clean without any visible oil leaks.

If you're in the UK, you should also check the car's MOT history and make sure that the DVLA's information matches the information you've been given. If you have a friend or relative with a good knowledge of cars, allow them to see the car.

Registering a car

Once you have bought a car, you need to register it. This process will depend on where you live. Each country or state has its own laws, so research what is required in your area. Motor car dealers should also be able to advise you, and some may even help you register the car.

For the USA: Check your local DMV website for information. You will need a Bill of Sale or a letter from the seller with details of the car make and model, year of manufacture, the selling price, and the car's VIN (Vehicle Identification Number), proof of insurance, a valid driver's license, proof of identity and birthdate, a Sales Tax Clearance certificate or money to pay for the sales tax at registration, a safety certificate, an emissions inspection certificate, the completed registration application form, and the registration fee.

For the UK: You must register the car with the local DVLA. Often the dealer will do this for you. A sales receipt, proof of valid insurance, an MOT certificate if the car is older than three years, completed paperwork, and the registration fee is needed. After about four weeks, you will be issued a vehicle log book (V5C).

Other countries: All countries require you to have proof of the sale, details of the car, a valid driver's license, completed paperwork, and the fee. Other requirements may vary.

Insurance

By law, all car owners must have insurance, which is a financial safeguard in case of an accident resulting in damage or injury to another person, vehicle, property, or animal. This type of insurance is called third-party coverage.

Shop around for insurance by getting quotes from two or three providers because prices will vary depending on your circumstances. The information that the insurance provider will need to quote is the make and model of the car, the year of manufacture, the age of the driver and when a driver's license was first obtained, where the car will be parked overnight and during the day and an estimate of how far you are likely to drive each month.

The jargon used by insurance providers:

Premium – the fee that you will pay each month.

Excess – when you claim from insurance, they will deduct a fee against each claim.

Broker – the person that will help you set up the insurance and make claims. Many insurance companies give you the option to deal directly with them, which saves some money as you are not also paying an intermediary.

Claim – if you have an accident or have significant expenses on your car, they will pay you out depending on what type of insurance you took.

Policy – the document they issue which sets out what your responsibilities are and what their responsibilities are. Always keep a copy.

MAINTENANCE OF YOUR CAR

Cars are a bit like pets – they need lots of care and attention.

Filling in Gas/Petrol

Did you know?

Approximately $85 000 is spent on gas during the lifetime of a motorist. That is over £65 000 for the average British motorist.

Considering the amount we spend on fuel, it's worthwhile to understand more information and do it right.

The quality of gasoline is measured with octane levels. The higher the octane number, the better the gasoline can resist knocking or pinging in an engine, leading to improved performance and fuel efficiency.

Your owner's manual will tell you what octane rating your car needs.

A number represents the octane rating, usually 87 (regular gasoline), 88-90 (mid-grade gasoline), and 91-94 (premium gasoline).

In the United Kingdom, the most commonly available gasoline octane ratings are 95 (known as "Super Unleaded") and 97 (known as "Premium Unleaded"). Some fuel stations may also offer 91 (known as "Unleaded") and diesel.

It's important to note that the UK's octane ratings may differ from those in other countries. It's always best to check the vehicle owner's manual for the recommended fuel type and octane rating.

It's important to know about octane ratings because using a fuel with a lower octane rating than recommended by the vehicle manufacturer can cause engine damage and decrease performance. On the other hand, using a higher octane fuel than needed does not provide any noticeable benefit and is a waste of money.

Top Tip

Most new vehicles manufactured in the past few decades clearly indicate which side the fuel tank is located on. Take a look at the fuel gauge display on your car's dashboard. You will find a symbol of a gasoline pump with an arrow. The direction the arrow points towards is the side of the car where the fuel filler cap is situated. In case your car doesn't have a fuel gauge arrow, you can still figure out which side the fuel filler cap is on by observing the gas pump symbol. The side where the hose is in the gas pump image indicates the location of the fuel filler cap.

An example of a fuel gauge display with the arrow indicating that the fuel filler cap is on the right.

To fill the fuel- use the hand brake and switch off the engine. Insert a credit card or pay inside the shop at the gas station. In some countries, there are fuel pump attendants who will help you, but mostly you will need to do this yourself. Open the fuel cap and lift the nozzle of the fuel pump. Select the octane level you need and insert the nozzle into the fuel tank. Squeeze the nozzle and fill the tank slowly using slow mode. When you have the nozzle firmly in place, face away from the tank so as not to breathe in fumes. Some pumps have an automatic shut-off system when fuel reaches a certain level. Do not keep pumping after this point. Once the tank is full, replace the nozzle on the gas pump. Replace the cap and close the door.

Top Tip

Fill up with fuel when the gauge gets to halfway. This will ensure that you do not run out of fuel. Also, check the pressure in the tires and the oil level while at the gas/petrol station.

Oil change

Always ensure that you have sufficient oil in the car. Check this before driving the car far away while the engine is still cool. Pull out the dipstick, wipe it off with a paper towel, and reinsert it. Now pull it out again and check the level. The dipstick has indicators on it to show when the level is low. Add a pint or two of oil if necessary.

After driving for about 5000 to 7500 miles, you need to change the oil in your car. You can save a lot of money by doing this yourself. Here's how to do this:

1. *Collect everything you need:* Work in old clothes and use a sheet of plastic about 2m x 2m to protect the garage floor or driveway paving. Buy sufficient car engine oil to fill the oil chamber. (The owner's manual will tell you the capacity). You will also need a new oil filter, a funnel, an oil pan for the old oil to

drain, a jack, a wrench, wheel blocks, or something to secure the wheels from rolling.

2. *Warm the oil slightly:* Start the car and allow it to run for about 5 minutes to warm the oil slightly.

3. *Set up your workspace:* Place the plastic sheet on the ground and drive the car over it. Engage the handbrake. Place the wheel blocks behind the back tires and then place the oil pan directly under the sump. Put the jack in position and crank it up to raise the vehicle so you can work under it. Leave the jack in place, and be careful not to bump it.

4. *Get to work:* Slide under the car and loosen the oil plug with the wrench. Allow the oil to drain into the pan. Remove the oil filter together with the old gasket (the rubber ring) on the rim and insert the new one. You can run a little oil around the rim of the new oil filter gasket to help it seal well. Ensure it is securely in place and tighten it with the wrench, but do not overtighten. When the oil has drained completely, refit the plug. Lower the car and remove the jack.

5. *Refill with clean oil:* Now pour sufficient new oil into the oil chamber from the top of the engine using the funnel. Allow it to settle for 15 minutes, and then check the level.

Washer fluid refill

To fill the windshield washer fluid reservoir of your car with new water, follow these steps:

1. Locate the windshield washer fluid reservoir: It is usually under the car's hood and has a cap labeled "windshield washer fluid."
2. Open the cap: Use a cloth to prevent dirt and grime from contaminating the fluid.
3. Fill the reservoir with water: Use a funnel to pour the water into the reservoir. Avoid using tap water, as it may contain minerals that can clog the washer fluid system. Use distilled water instead.
4. Check the level: Ensure the fluid level is at the "full" line after filling.
5. Replace the cap: Close the cap securely.

Note: Some cars may have a different type of washer fluid, such as an antifreeze solution, and it's essential to use the type recommended by the manufacturer. Check your car owner's manual for more information.

Coolant refill

Here is a step-by-step guide on how to refill the engine coolant in your car:

1. Locate the coolant reservoir: It is usually a clear plastic tank near the engine and has the word "Coolant" or "Antifreeze" marked.

2. Determine the correct coolant: Check your car owner's manual to determine the type of coolant recommended for your vehicle. It's essential to use the right type to avoid damaging the engine.

3. Ensure the engine is cool: Engine coolant can be hot and pressurized, so it's important to wait until the engine has cooled down before removing the coolant reservoir cap.

4. Remove the cap: Slowly unscrew the cap to release pressure and remove it completely.

5. Check the level: If the coolant level is low, add more coolant to the reservoir until it reaches the "full" line.

6. Replace the cap: Put it back on the coolant reservoir and tighten it securely.

7. Start the engine: Let it run for a few minutes to circulate the new coolant throughout the system.

8. Check for leaks: Check for leaks around the coolant reservoir and hoses.

Keeping the engine coolant at the proper level is important to avoid overheating and potential engine damage. It's also a good idea to check the coolant level regularly by a professional mechanic.

Responsible driving

Are you excited about having a driver's license and a car of your own? Having the freedom and independence to go where you want to, when you want to, really 'slaps,' but you need to be 'dank' about this, so you live longer.

Traffic rules

Traffic rules are actually rules and not just suggestions. They are there to keep everyone safe! You had to learn them and apply them to get your license, so just make a pact with yourself not to abandon what you have learned.

Did you know?

On average, an accident is likely to happen 3 seconds after the driver is distracted.

Keep these guidelines in mind while driving:

- NEVER drink and drive – not even for a short distance.
- Keep to the speed limit – arriving late is better than not arriving at all.
- Buckle up and ensure that your passengers do so too.
- Always wear a helmet when riding a motorbike.
- Never allow yourself to become distracted.
- Keep calm and drive safely – if you are angry or agitated, take a few minutes to calm down before getting behind the steering wheel of a car.

Here is an anecdote to show how important it is to avoid being distracted. A newly licensed driver swerved off the side of the road very shortly after leaving the testing ground. When asked what happened, he sheepishly admitted that he had been distracted by messages on his phone. His friends were checking whether he had passed his test. Sadly, this type of accident happens often, but since you are truly on your way to being an independent and responsible adult, you'll know to avoid this.

Enjoy greater freedom from being able to travel around on your own. You are now fully prepared to follow maps and transport timetables and know how to maintain your own vehicle and what to do if you have a breakdown.

6

MAKING A GOOD IMPRESSION

Ever heard the expression, "Don't judge a book by its cover," meaning what you see first is not the whole story? Well, while that is true, psychologists also warn that a first impression will last whether it is accurate or not.

Dame Natalie Massenet, a British-American fashion entrepreneur and Founder of the designer fashion portal Net-a-Porter says, "Never forget that you only have one opportunity to make a first impression – with investors, with customers, with PR, and with marketing."

SO HOW DO YOU MAKE A GOOD IMPRESSION?

- Smile warmly and openly

144 | KYLA MILLER

- Make eye contact with the person you are talking to
- Dress appropriately for the event
- Communicate well by speaking clearly and audibly
- Listen more than you speak
- Be authentically you
- Have empathy for others; everyone has challenges.
- Control your body language, especially if you are feeling negative emotions
- Prepare well – get as much information as you can and then rehearse what you need to say
- Be flexible if necessary
- Show confidence.

Let's look at the most important of these points – Communication and listening.

COMMUNICATION SKILLS

It is always best to communicate with people face-to-face. This way, you can see their reaction to what you are saying. If they look puzzled, you'll know to explain in more depth. If they look tense, you'll know they are not yet on board with what you are saying, and you may need to be more persuasive or give them more information. When you text, email, or talk over the phone, body language is absent, so you need to listen more clearly to words, tone of voice, and pace of delivery. These are clues. If the person is hesitant or the tone is icy, you will need to work at communicating to prevent the possibility of a misunderstanding.

No doubt, as a child, you played broken telephone. That's an excellent example of how communication can get distorted. Never assume that the receiver of your message knows what you mean. Here's an example:

While Kyle was trying to complete his chemistry assignment, a snowstorm hit. Suddenly his computer froze, and he called out to his dad, "Window's frozen and won't open." His dad was puzzled about why he would want to open the window in the cold weather but called out, "Pour some hot water over it, then it will work." Kyle asked his dad if he was sure that was how to deal with it. Turning his attention back to the telly, his dad called, "Yes, that will definitely work!" About ten minutes later, Kyle went to his dad and said, "Dad, I did what you told me to, but now my computer won't even turn on, and I must get my assignment done." His dad finally went upstairs to look and realized his mistake – Kyle had been talking about the operating system on the computer, not the windows to ventilate the room.

While the above story probably isn't true because Kyle is savvier than that, it illustrates the importance of being clear when communicating. Never assume that the listener knows what you are talking about.

Did you know?

Communication is a basic loop: the sender sends a message the receiver receives. He/she interprets the message and sends a new one back.

Unfortunately, it's actually a bit more complicated than that. There is interference between sending and receiving, which can disrupt the communication loop. Interference can be anything like noise from the telly, distracted attention, past experiences, or a lack of facts or information.

With Kyle and his dad, there was a distraction, lack of information, and noise from the telly resulting in a disaster.

WE ARE ALL DIFFERENT

So why is communication so complicated? The simple answer is that you are different from the people around you. This is a good thing! The things you like or dislike, your sense of humor, the way you look and move, the clothes you choose, and the things you are interested in all combine to make you who you are.

Top Tip

Research various personality types. This will give you information on how to communicate more effectively. You can also do online quizzes or tests to see your personality type, giving you insight into your personality.

There are various personality types theories, all of which are valid. One of the most common theories divides people into these four groups. You are a combination of the following:

Choleric: Outgoing, natural leader, logical, analytical, focused

Melancholic: Deep thinker, emotional, sensitive to others, paying attention to detail

Phlegmatic: Careful, seemingly reluctant, avoiding change and conflict, thorough

Sanguine: Friendly, optimistic, carefree, and easy to approach.

No one fits the above categories exactly, and you will be a combination of each category to varying degrees.

HOW DO YOU TALK TO PEOPLE?

Think about how you like people to talk to you and what makes you angry when others talk to you. No one wants to be bossed around or spoken to rudely. It's all about self-control and respect for others. Remember, it's usually not your fault if someone reacts to you. Often, they are battling with something that may be overwhelming, tired, not well, or distracted. Try not to get upset and to respond respect-fully still.

HOW DO YOU LISTEN WELL AND GET PEOPLE TO LISTEN TO YOU?

- Show acceptance of the speaker.
- Be open to what they have to say by tuning in and hearing not only the words but the tone of voice and the pace at which they speak.
- Check your emotions. If you get angry or upset, you can say, "I need to think about this; let's talk again later." When you are calm, re-initiate the conversation.
- Watch your body language – keep it positive with a nod of the head, eye contact, or leaning in slightly.
- Use a person's name when you talk to them. This shows that you care for and respect them.
- Seek to understand and ensure that the other person understands you.
- You can summarize the conversation to show that you have heard it correctly.
- Eliminate distractions as far as possible.
- Avoid interrupting.
- Try to see the situation from the other person's point of view.

Social media influencer and international bestselling author Bryant H. McGill said, "*One of the most sincere forms of respect is actually listening to what another has to say.*"

Did you know?

The Chinese symbol for "listening" comprises two main characters; one shows the ears, and the other shows the heart. This perfectly illustrates how important it is to listen well to truly hear the 'core' message.

NEGOTIATING A WIN-WIN

Consider the 5 P's of negotiating using a real-life scenario: You have arranged to take your girlfriend on a date on Saturday at 6.30 pm, and you need to borrow your mom's car. She has agreed to meet her friend at the local mall at 7 pm to go to the movies and also needs her car.

Prepare

1. Get information on communicating with the other person and what they are likely to want (Avoid discussing this while your mom is busy or stressed)

2. Think about what you would like the ultimate solution to look like (You want the car for an unlimited time)

3. Explore all the options available to you and the other person. (You could drop her off, get her to pay for alternative transport, or change the day or time of your date)

Probe

While talking to the other person, try to find out what they want or what they will be willing to do or give to find a solution (Ask your mom what her plans are, and suggest some alternatives: either one of you needs to change the date and time of your outing; either one of you pays for expensive transport)

Possibilities

Talk through the possibilities, examine the pros and cons, and determine what each person will be willing to bring to solve the problem (Transport is too expensive; you both have pre-arranged activities and are bound by when other people are available)

Propose

Clearly verbalize the solution. This may take some backward and forward discussion until both people are happy (Propose dropping your mom off at her friend's house at 6.30 pm and getting her friend to bring her back home after the movies)

Partner

Do what you can to collaborate and make the solution work (The solution meant changing the time of your date from 6.30 pm to 7 pm, but that was a small sacrifice to make since you have the car for as long as you need it.

Congratulations on negotiating a win-win solution.

FORMS OF COMMUNICATION

The various forms of communication are used for specific purposes:

Writing - When it is necessary to have a record of the discussion, or when the message is one-sided, it is best to use written communication. This can be a letter, meeting minutes, report, email, or social media posts.

Always read through what you have written and use available tools to check the grammar and spelling. Remember to be very clear and give all the necessary details. (Remember Kyle and his dad? There would have been no misunderstanding if Kyle had mentioned that the Windows *program on his computer* had frozen).

The subject or heading on written communication should clearly indicate what the topic is going to be. Think how you would like it labeled if you were to have to find the email in a day or two. What subject line would be helpful?

Talking – Any situation where discussion is needed should first be done by talking. This discussion method is much quicker than sending written communication back and forth several times.

Non-verbal – There are always clues to be picked up by body language, facial expressions, or chosen surroundings.

SOCIAL SKILLS AND MANNERS

Dr. Craig Sawchuk, a Mayo Clinic Psychologist, recently wrote a blog stating that socializing helps to combat feelings of loneliness, helps to sharpen memory and cognitive skills, and generally increases well-being and happiness, ultimately causing humans to live longer. When asked how you can best socialize, he went on to say that in-person connecting is best, although connecting via technology is better than not connecting at all.

DEVELOPING HOBBIES AND INTERESTS

Think about what you are interested in. Take note of what websites you access, what topics you enjoy researching, and what you spend your time thinking about. These are the things that you are interested in. There are many groups, clubs, and courses that you can join where you can develop your skills and meet people that have similar interests to you.

DEVELOP AND MAINTAIN FRIENDSHIPS

Friendships and family relationships don't just happen; they need to be cultivated and nurtured. The more time you spend with a person, the more you get to know them and value them for who they are. This is where authenticity is essential. Be with someone because you like them, not because you can get something from them.

Relationships can be tricky, especially with people you did not necessarily choose to be with, like family or colleagues. Honest communication delivered calmly and respectfully is vital. Respecting each others' point of view is more important than being right.

HEALTHY FAMILY RELATIONSHIPS

The more time you spend with someone, the more carefully you need to handle the relationship. Strained relationships with family, friends, and colleagues can be very stressful, and these relationships need extra care.

Never be too proud to say, "I'm sorry," especially if you are wrong or have messed up. Forgiveness is a very powerful and effective way to mend relationships. Although you can't change what has happened in the past, you can choose to let go of your anger and not hold on to grudges.

While saying sorry comes naturally to some of us, and we can't relax until we have done so, the rest of us may feel ashamed, guilty, and inadequate when apologizing. Apologizing is not a sign of weakness; it is simply a way of building a bridge to restore a relationship and set boundaries for the future.

SO WHY SHOULD YOU APOLOGIZE?

It may seem like you are losing face when apologizing, but actually, you will gain the following:

- A deeper understanding of each other can develop.
- Having boundaries within a relationship leads to healthier interaction.
- It restores dignity to the hurt person, letting them know that you care about their feelings.
- It opens up an opportunity to talk again and restore the connection.
- It mends trust, which is a very valuable part of honest relationships.
- It shows that you are self-aware and mature.

An apology should always be sincere and honest to prevent more damage. Keep it simple by acknowledging what you did wrong and how it must have made the person feel. Suggest what you can do to help resolve the issue and remember to ask the other person if they have an idea of what to do going forward to prevent the situation from happening again. An example is, "I am sorry that I shouted at you; it must have sounded harsh and uncaring and hurt your feelings. From now on, I will try to discuss issues more calmly. Do you have a suggestion on how we can resolve this?"

Don't use the opportunity to criticize or belittle the other person or get your point across at all costs. Avoid making promises that you will not be able to keep. If you still need to resolve the issue, wait until everyone's emotions have settled, and then find a constructive way to deal with the problem calmly.

Jade and her friend Eleanor were chatting and joking when Jade began teasing Eleanor about her boyfriend, Jack. Without thinking, Jade makes a comment criticizing Jack for not paying enough attention to Eleanor. Eleanor got very upset, stood up, and walked away. "You idiot," shouted Jade, "I'm just joking." Later in the day, Jade realized that Eleanor had chosen to sit on the opposite side of the lecture hall instead of next to her. "What's up with Eleanor?" she thought. Suddenly it dawned on her that Eleanor had left in the middle of their conversation earlier, so she began to think through what they had been talking about. Then she remembered what she had said about Jack and how it had probably hurt Eleanor, even though it was true. Jack did not pay as much attention to her as she would have liked, and she had confided this to Jade a few days earlier. Jade realized she had hurt her friend badly by teasing her and calling her an idiot. After the lecture, Jade ensured she crossed paths with Eleanor and asked if they could talk. At first, Eleanor was icy and stiff. Jade said, "Eleanor, I am truly sorry for my comment about Jack. It must have hurt you, and the last thing I want to do is cause you more pain. I'm also sorry for calling you an 'idiot' and for being so insensitive. In the future, I will be more careful with the information you confide in me and be more supportive of your relationship with Jack." Two weeks later, Jade was able to have an honest but kind talk with Eleanor to express her concern over the way that Jack treated Eleanor. It went well, and Eleanor took Jade's advice.

Basic politeness

While it's never okay to be rude to someone, being rude to a stranger you will never see again will have little impact on your life, although it will impact theirs. But being disrespectful to colleagues or family will have long-lasting repercussions. These relationships can deteriorate quickly and are very difficult to repair. Treat everyone you meet with the same respect you would like to receive from them, especially family.

In general, people respond better to politeness. If you need something, say 'please' before you state what they can help with. Always thank people when they have assisted you. Before engaging in conversation, greet the other person and look them in the eye. If you are engaging with them for more than just a brief moment, it is also appropriate to introduce yourself and allow them to do the same.

Respect the opinions and views of others, whether they match your own or not. Sometimes you may meet someone whose views or opinion is completely opposite to what you believe. Keep these points in mind, and you will find it easier to engage with them:

- Keep an open mind. They may have a valid point.
- Try to find and focus on the things that you have in common.
- Listen to them anyway so that they will also be open to what you have to say when you express your view.
- Keep your emotions under control. Do not show intolerance.
- Try to understand what may have brought them to form their opinion.

Remember that your true character is shown in the way that you treat others.

ENTERTAINING AND PARTYING

All of us will host parties at some point to celebrate a milestone or achievement or just to hang out with friends.

As the host:

Whether you are planning a party long in advance or spontaneously inviting friends over, be sure to give precise details. Give your guests a definite time, date, and venue address. They also need to know if the party is for a special occasion, whether they should bring something and what to wear. Arriving out of sync or being dressed differently from everyone else will make your guest uncomfortable. The more relaxed you and your guests are, the more successful your party will be.

Pay attention to the details. Whether you plan to have a sit-down meal or a picnic, plan the food, setting, and surrounding atmosphere well. This will ensure that you are relaxed.

Greet your guests warmly and make sure throughout the event that they are comfortable and have what they need – something to drink and eat. If you notice that one guest is left out of the conversation, find a way to include them.

Be flexible and adapt easily if necessary. Sometimes things can go wrong, but don't let this tense you; try to find alternate plans or have a good laugh.

As a guest:

Being a guest also carries some responsibility for the success of the event. Always reply to invitations by letting your host know whether you will attend. Arrive on time or within ten minutes of the stated time. If you are going to be late, let your host know.

Do what you can to participate in the conversation and activities and assist your host by passing around drinks and food to other guests. Ensure that no one is left out but that all guests are included. Be moderate in the food and drink you consume, and thank your host when you leave.

THE WORLD OF WORK

As you grow older, new opportunities will open up for you, one of which is the ability to earn an income. While gaining this independence and freedom is exciting, it comes with new and seemingly scary responsibilities.

Communication skills at work

Clearly, communicating in a work environment is essential and requires practice. You may be required to report back to a meeting or give a presentation. Although some companies will provide you with training, this may not necessarily be the case, so it is vital to upskill yourself. Do the research, and then get some practice armed with this new knowledge. Speak in front of your mirror at home to practice, observe yourself, and build confidence.

Here are some suggestions for communicating in various scenarios at work:

In-person face to face meetings:

This is the best way to hold meetings, although it may seem the scariest. Ensure the details, such as time, venue, and purpose of the meeting, are clear. Arrive at least 5 minutes before the session is due to start. If you are hosting the meeting, ensure everything is in place before the meeting is scheduled to start. Check the computer and screen, the number of chairs so everyone can sit, arrange refreshments, etc. Inform the receptionist about the meeting so that she/he is prepared and knows what to do when people arrive. Try to begin the meeting on time and stick to the purpose of the meeting. Only bring up relevant topics. When you need to speak, do so boldly and confidently so that everyone can hear you clearly. Make notes beforehand to make your contribution to the meeting logical and clear. Try to answer questions directly. Suppose you are unsure of the answer; state that you will find out and get back to the person. Make sure you do so with a follow-up email to all who attended the meeting.

Online meetings:

These are similar to the above, except that you must position your computer and camera correctly and check your background and microphone beforehand. Always make sure that a professional impression is left on the other attendees. If you are working from home out of your bedroom, insert a neutral background screen using the tools on the software you are using. If that is not possible, ensure that your room is tidy and there is a shelf, window, or door behind you rather than an unmade bed. Be aware that noises carry and keep your microphone muted until you speak.

Telephone conversations:

Spoken words and the tone of your voice are the only way to communicate in this setting, so you must say exactly what you mean. The other person does not have the ability to read your body language or hand gestures as additional indicators. Keep the conversation short and follow up with an email to summarize the discussion and confirm the details. Speak clearly and be aware of background noises that may carry. If you are in an open office, let your colleagues know that you will need some quiet for 5 minutes before you make the call.

Emails:

People are busy and do not like to read long emails. Keep to one introductory sentence and a paragraph or two to say what you need to say. Finish with a 'call to action' or short sentence on what you expect the recipient to do and give a reasonable deadline. You should only deal with one topic at a time. Use the subject line to state what the topic is clearly.

Whatsapp/SMS:

Only use this communication method in a business environment if the other person has indicated that this is their preferred method. Keep the message short with only the essential details, and if necessary, follow up with an email giving more information or an attachment.

Practice writing reports, emails, and other documents, and take note of the style in which the company writes. Some companies write formally, while others use a more relaxed way of expressing things.

Thinking and analytical skills

Mostly you will be expected to work in a team with others, but you will need to contribute ideas and help solve problems when they arise. Try to look at the task you have been given from as many various points of view as possible. For example, if you are on the team developing a new product, think about the following: Who will use the product? What will they want it to do? What result will they expect? How much can they pay? Is it easy to store? Some of the most useful analytical skills can be developed:

- Look at specific details of a project and try to notice unique patterns and features.
- Research as much as possible about the product or project, looking at past models and competitors' products.
- Think about the future impact of the product on society, the environment, the economy, and so on.
- Use your imagination about what the ideal solution would be. Ask 'what if' and devise solutions no one else has thought of.
- Try to see the different parts of a project or product separately. Then look at how they interact with each other.
- Divide the information you gained while researching into categories to evaluate how things fit together or oppose one another.

- Try to make predictions about the impact of decisions that are taken.

Work ethic

Developing a solid work ethic is key to retaining your job and getting promoted. At the very least, you should arrive before work is due to start so that you are at your desk with the computer logged on at starting time. Only pack up after the time at which work is due to finish. If your team is under pressure to complete a project, offer to work extra hours or help another struggling team member. When you are at work, focus only on work and complete tasks as quickly and thoroughly as possible. Avoid taking and making private phone calls and social chats that have nothing to do with the task at hand.

Integrity

This is probably one of the most important attributes needed in the business world. Always be honest, dependable, and morally sound. Your teammates need to know that they can trust you.

Life-long learning

You will never know everything there is to learn, so continually increase your skills, knowledge, and experience. This prevents boredom and helps you to build your career. Because technology is constantly evolving and new things are being discovered, it's important to continually refresh your knowledge and keep up to date with changes in your industry.

Owning your strengths and weaknesses

Self-awareness will help you to grow and develop. Your strengths are what make you good at something. Weaknesses are simply areas that need to be worked at to improve or develop. For instance, if you find it challenging to do presentations at work, seek opportunities to build your confidence when talking to people. Start by just greeting the cashiers at the local shops. Once more comfortable with this, speak to a colleague on a coffee break. When you are satisfied, volunteer to do the team report at the next meeting. Soon you will gain the confidence to stand up and do a presentation.

STAY SAFE ONLINE: WHAT IS A STRONG PASSWORD?

It's one that you can easily remember, but no one else will figure out. Never use names, birthdates, locations, consecutive numbers, or alphabetical letters. A strong password combines letters in uppercase and lowercase, numbers, and special characters. Try some of the following:

- Leave out the vowels of your favorite movie title
- Substitute vowels with special characters in the name of your favorite band

- Substitute some consonants with special characters in your grandmother's maiden name
- Misspell a word made up of a phrase from song lyrics.

Even though you already know this, repeating and reminding you is essential. NEVER give your password to anyone. You would never give a thief the key to your house, so make sure you keep your password safe.

Also, be careful of what you post online – it becomes indelible and can never be entirely deleted.

Using a VPN

This masks your IP address so you cannot be tracked, and some VPNs also encrypt your data, allowing you to browse anonymously, reducing the chance of being cyberstalked.

Research your options thoroughly, as each country has access to various VPNs. Choose a VPN that is:

- Easy to use
- Covers all your digital devices
- Has good customer support
- Is closest to your physical location
- Is on the recommended list for your country
- Has 256-bit AES, DNS/IPv6 leak protection, kill switch, and split tunneling.

When you have chosen and downloaded a VPN, you can connect it by typing your router's IP (Internet Protocol) address and password to log into your admin panel. The VPN options should display in the settings, and you can select the client option. Enter the correct settings and then follow any other prompts the router indicates.

Safe banking

Always use the official app or internet portal from your bank. Usually, your bank will require you to go into the branch to set this up initially. When doing online banking, make sure that you complete all transactions before walking away from your computer and double-check that you have closed the app or website when you are finished.

Avoid giving away information

Always check the details in photo backgrounds when posting online to ensure that you are not giving away your location or personal information. Avoid street signs, shop names, or easily identifiable landmarks; never state where you are or will be going. Post photos at least twenty four hours after you have left an identifiable area.

Identity theft

All documents with personal information should be shredded and not just thrown away. Tearing these papers up is not good enough as they can be collected and pieced together to gather your information.

Getting back up or help

No matter how careful you are, you can get cyberstalked. This can happen when someone you do not know or barely know follows you on social media without your knowledge to gain information about what you are doing or where you are going. Only accept invitations to social media platforms if you personally know and have met the person. While it's a good idea to have your own parents as 'friends' or 'followers' on social media, be very careful about adding the parents of friends or classmates.

Immediately let your parents know if any comments or suggestions make you feel uncomfortable. You are NOT to blame and should not feel guilty. The inappropriate adult or older teenager is at fault and needs to be called out and dealt with.

As you approach adulthood, you are more and more responsible for your behavior. A mature person can communicate well and control emotions, or at least moderate when to display appropriate emotion. The impression you give will be how you are viewed going forward, and it is very difficult to change perceptions. Conscientiously develop respect for others, integrity, and a good work ethic, and you will create a good impression of yourself and make a success of your life.

7

RESOLVE ISSUES EASILY

Moving away from home and setting up your own home gives you the opportunity to take control of your own life. You get to decide how you want to live it. Intentionally and successfully or indifferently with random results? You can choose how you want to respond to the world around you.

Israelmore Ayivor, author, blogger, and motivational speaker, says, *"If you manage yourself, you control the flow of your time in the right direction. It takes self-discipline to be at the center of control for your own time."*

COPING SKILLS

Self-control is about choosing your responses, while self-management is an overall concept of steering yourself in the direction you want to go. It's all about taking responsibility for your behavior and an essential skill for getting ahead in the world. You choose whether to react impulsively to situations or respond with positive solutions.

The benefits of self-management

Daniel had a temper and quickly reacted to anything he did not like by punching, kicking, or throwing things around, causing damage to the doors, walls, and windows of his bedroom. One day his father had had enough, and when Daniel finally calmed down, he removed all Daniel's belongings from the room, telling him that he could have them back when he had repaired the walls, door, and window. Daniel looked around the empty room and realized how much damage he had done. His father explained that the next time he flew into a rage, he should use the energy to do something good such as patching the walls. Sure enough, the next time Daniel flew into a frenzy, his father pushed the tin of wall-filler and a blunt pallet knife through the door. Eventually, Daniel calmed down, and because he was bored, he patched the walls of his room. The very next time he got into a rage, his father quietly handed him the tools to repair the door's broken lock, replace the glass in the window, and so on. Daniel quickly concluded that if he channeled his energy into doing something, he felt much better and less angry. After about a week, his room was repaired, and all his belongings were returned. Now, when Daniel gets angry, he runs, grabs a skipping rope to work off the energy, or rakes up the leaves in the yard. He has realized that although he has little control over his feelings, he can control how he expresses his feelings and that finding a positive outlet for his emotions helps him to feel better and has great benefits. Other benefits of learning self-control are:

- Positively focused energy can be productive.
- The feeling of helplessness is reduced.
- Relationships with family, friends, and co-workers will be better.
- Mental health will be improved because there will be less inner turmoil.
- Physical health is better due to more positive activities.
- Emotions are acknowledged without them controlling bad behavior.
- There is an opportunity to learn about your strengths and weaknesses.
- Sleep is better quality because you are calmer.

Be your own manager

Manage your changes:

It's a fact that change rocks your world, and you need to rebalance and recalibrate. Give yourself time to do so. Immediately after a change in where you live or work, let yourself slowly ease into the new environment. Have you ever thrown a stone into a pool of water and watched the ripples that formed? You will have noticed that the rings closest to where the stone landed are the most visible, and as the ripples spread outward, they become less definite. Use this illustration to manage your changes. Starting with the ripple closest to you - your home or relationships. Take time to unpack and arrange your belongings in a way that gives you comfort. Next, investigate your neighborhood by going for a short walk. Then find the local shops, venturing out a little further each time. Next, explore your work environment, and get to know the people on your team. Eventually, you can also get to know other team members and explore the options of extra activities in a hobby group.

Manage your emotions:

Never suppress emotions by denying that they are there or delaying an opportunity to express them. This is very unhealthy in the long term. Instead, learn to express your emotions positively or appropriately channel them. Remember how Daniel learned to use all that negative energy to achieve something positive? Place a label on your emotions - anger, frustration, happiness, joy and then learn to express your emotions by talking about how you feel or by physically working off the energy or intensity. Instead of having an angry outburst at work, take a break, walk around the block, or run after work. Remember that positive emotions also need an outlet. Sing a song in the shower or dance to your favorite music.

Manage your responses:

Learn to respond rather than react: Reactions are immediate without thought, while responses are delayed until you can appropriately express the emotions. It is not appropriate to shout at your co-worker in the middle of a team meeting because it humiliates them, and others are drawn into the drama, which escalates the problem. Control your response and emotions until after the meeting, and then once you have calmed down, you can schedule a time to discuss how to handle the situation best with your co-worker. Remember, it is always better to do nothing than to do the wrong thing!

Manage your time:

It is incredible how much can be done in a short amount of time. Five minutes of dusting at home will make a big difference to the general cleanliness of your home. Activities can be combined to save time. The bus ride home typically takes 30 minutes, and then you still need to go for a 30-minute walk later in the evening, taking up 1 hour of your time. But, walking home instead of riding the bus takes up a total of 40 minutes. You have saved 20 minutes extra to study and save yourself some money.

Next time you need to get a few groceries, try stopping at the shop on the way home if you pass it instead of going back later. Because you are not going backward and forwards on the same route, you will save time.

Manage your priorities:

Focusing on what's most important will help you juggle the many tasks you have and get everything done on time. To decide which tasks are a priority, list all you must do. Then add a column and write down what will happen if you ignore the task. Here is an example:

Tasks to complete	Outcome if not done	Importance
College assignment	Fail	Priority
Application to write exam	Fail	Priority
Laundry	Still have clean clothes	Postpone to 2 days time
Grocery shopping	Can eat leftovers in the fridge	Postpone to tomorrow

In the last column, you can see which tasks are a priority and which can be rescheduled or postponed.

Managing loneliness:

Building new relationships takes time. Don't be afraid to be on your own sometimes. It's an excellent opportunity to get to know yourself. But, if you find yourself feeling sad or you are spending too much time alone, you can try one of the following tips:

- Join a club that offers activities that you are interested in
- Get a part-time job – this is a great way to connect with people
- Attend social events such as work functions or on-campus activities
- Take up a sport that you enjoy
- Connect with your family or friends using a video app so that you can see them as well as hear them
- Form a study group that will connect you with people and helps you study.
- Don't be afraid to admit that you feel loneliness – it's a normal human feeling.

PROBLEM-SOLVING SKILLS

Because everybody is different, there are also different responses to problems or stressful situations. For example, you and your co-workers are working on an important exhibition at the local Convention Center. Your boss has emphasized how important this event is for the company and insisted that everything is perfect. Two days before the event, there is a fire at the venue, and your team leader receives a call to say that the exhibition cannot go ahead. Each team member has a different reaction:

Team Member A *freezes* up, becoming tense and silent, and can't speak up to make suggestions on how to solve the problem. Team Member B *fights*, banging a fist on the desk and shouting loudly. Team Member C has an entirely different response and takes *flight* by leaving the office building and her co-workers to work it out for themselves. Team Member D *flops,* puts his head on the desk, and goes to sleep, avoiding the situation. While Team Member E thinks for a while and then picks up his phone and calls a *friend* to find out the name and contact number of the venue, his company used the previous week for their exhibition.

None of these responses were wrong. They are natural reactions that different people have. The trick is to get to know how you react in a crisis. Acknowledge your natural reaction, and then learn to manage yourself so that you can face the problem to solve it.

Steps to solving problems

State the problem - Define the problem in one or two sentences. It may help to write it (Find a new venue)

Expand the problem - Add other important information (Notify exhibitors of the change of venue; Send out updated venue information to the public)

Set timelines - Decide by when you need to get the solution into effect (By the end of the day)

Identify the root cause - If a problem keeps recurring deal with what causes it (Check safety specifications at the new venue so the problem is not repeated)

Develop an action plan - Write down a sequence of what needs to be done (Start phoning all exhibitors; Arrange the delivery of goods to the new venue; Send out messages to the public on social media; Make posters to redirect attendees, etc.)

Execute the plan - As the plan is implemented, tick off the tasks and assign specific tasks to specific people (Assign tasks to team members: Team Member A can start phoning all exhibitors; Team Member B can arrange the delivery of goods to the new venue; Team Member C can send out messages to the public on social media; Team Member D can make posters to redirect attendees, etc.)

Evaluate the results - Make adjustments if necessary (Get the team members to report to the team leader as they complete each task and adjust when necessary)

Continuously improve – Monitor the team to see where improvements are needed (Help Team Member A phone exhibitors to speed up the process).

Effects of ongoing problems and stress

It is crucial to solving problems as they arise. Sometimes issues are quick and easy to solve, and we can move on, but often the same problem keeps recurring, especially if step four of the problem-solving formula above has not been effective. Ongoing issues can result in stress, eroding your body's immune system and making you constantly sick or depressed. You may feel anxious all the time and suffer from fatigue and headaches. Some people battle to sleep or overeat or turn to addictive substances to avoid their problems. Trouble concentrating creates further issues. Continual stress can lead to heart attacks, a stroke, or addiction.

How to manage stress

Sometimes problems take time to solve, so you must manage your stress levels while you work at solving the problem.

Find a balance: Make time to play in between working hard. Schedule time each week to do something you enjoy that will take your mind off the problem.

Stick with your routine: As far as possible, keep to your usual routine with meals and bedtimes at roughly the same time every day.

Make a plan: While your mind is distracted, write down what needs to be done, even the ordinary routine stuff, like packing lunch, dropping off keys, phoning mom, completing assignments, and doing laundry. This will prevent you from forgetting important tasks and creating more problems.

Ask for help: No one has to struggle through on their own. It shows maturity to be able to ask for help. Think about what you can outsource while you are under stress. Maybe dropping your clothes off at the local laundry on the way to work will help to give you more time to work on an overdue project. Or, getting a once-off pizza delivery will keep you

LIFE SKILLS FOR TEENS | 179

fed while you continue working at home to write an urgent report.

Work out the stress: Keeping up physical activity is essential. Go for a walk, a run, punch a punching bag, skip, etc. All that adrenalin in your body needs an outlet, or it will build up and cause health problems.

Prioritize: Focus on the most urgent tasks and make a note to do other jobs at a later stage. You may have planned to paint the wall this weekend, but now the problem with the fire at the exhibition center has you working all weekend. Postpone the painting to next weekend.

Lighten up: You will get through this crisis. Sometimes just having a good laugh helps. If you need to, read some jokes, or watch a funny comedy.

Think creatively: Approaching a problem from a different angle can also help. We can take an example from this cute tale. Twelve animals are hanging onto a rope that comes down from a tall tree. Eleven of them are monkeys, and one is a squirrel. They all decide that one animal should get off because if they don't, the rope will break, and all of them will fall. No one can decide who should go, so finally, the squirrel speaks up and delivers a very touching speech, ending with the words, "I'll get off." The monkeys, all moved by the squirrel's speech, start clapping and let the rope go. Problem solved.

Here's another example. My co-worker Samantha is always about 30 minutes late. Last week we had a very important presentation to attend at 10 o'clock at our branch in the next town, and she asked me for a lift. I told her that the presentation started at 9.30 and we had to leave by 9.10. She made a real effort and arrived just 15 minutes late. So, we only left at 9.25 but still got to the presentation by 9.50, which was plenty of time to find our seats and get settled and ready for the presentation's start. Problem solved

Breathe deeply: Your body needs oxygen, but when stressed, you tend to breathe less deeply, not filling your lungs with air. Place your hands across your tummy with the fingers loosely interwoven. Breathe while pushing out your tummy. Your fingertips should have moved apart if you breathed deeply enough. Hold your breath for about 10 seconds, then breathe out, sucking the tummy in. At first, it will seem odd to push your tummy out when breathing in and suck it in when breathing out, but this allows your lungs to fill to maximum capacity. Do this deep breathing four or five times each time and several times a day.

Drink water: This may sound odd, but the fact is that your body is made up of 60% water and functions better when it is well hydrated. Stress distracts you from doing what you usually do, so focus on drinking enough water.

Spirituality: A strong belief system can influence the way you see things and the values you accept or reject. It also gives a sense of belonging and can provide a much-needed support system. Psychologists acknowledge that people with strong belief systems cope better with problems.

DECISION-MAKING SKILLS

Every day you will be faced with having to make decisions: What to eat for breakfast, what to wear to the office, to watch the telly, or to do your assignment. These are simple decisions, and the results of your choices are unlikely to impact your life too seriously. (Except that assignment does need to be done, so switch off the telly...) But, there are some decisions that you are faced with that will impact your life seriously. When faced with these important decisions, such as what course to study, what career to follow, whether you should get married, and so on, it is mature and wise to get the input of someone else whom you can trust and who knows you well. Be patient and think through what they are saying before you discard their advice. These suggestions can help you to make decisions:

Analyze – Gather as much information as you possibly can. For example, if you are deciding on a career path, start with something you are interested in, and collect information on the possible jobs, the requirements to get the jobs, or what to study to equip yourself with the necessary skills.

Be creative – It often helps to look at options creatively or use your imagination. For example, you need to decide where to live. There are two apartments within your price range, and after making a list of all the positive and negative points, you still can't choose. Now's the time to get your creativity and imagination working. Picture how you will furnish and decorate apartment 1 - you can even do a design board, sketching out a rough diagram using colored pencils. Imagine relaxing there, preparing meals, sleeping, entertaining friends, etc. Now do the same for apartment 2. You are likely to feel drawn to one apartment over the other and able to make a decision.

Consider – Look at all the options open to you and consider the result each option will bring. Make a list of all the positive points (pros) and then all the negative points (cons) of Option 1. Repeat this process with Option 2, etc. Choose the option that gives you the most positives and the least negatives. This is the best solution.

Collaborate – Discuss the various options with someone you trust and know has some experience. Although the final decision rests with you, having their input or perspective will be helpful. Others may see potential pitfalls you can't see or never thought of. Their input can be constructive in pointing out potential pitfalls or successes and the various options.

Did you know?

There are five types of decision-makers:

Morris, the Motivator - likes to explore all the facts and get a realistic sense of each possible result.

Vikram, the Visionary - likes progress and is not afraid of change. He is happy to get the opinions and views of others to help make his decisions.

Finley Flexible is open-minded and adaptable to various outcomes, so he finds it challenging to make a decision and seldom gets to a decision quickly.

Gareth the Guardian - is not comfortable with change and making decisions. He will consider all the pros and cons to ensure that the decision is definitely the correct one.

Caty the Catalyst - prefers action and will quickly decide after briefly gathering information.

Which of these styles matches yours?

Now that you have some tools for managing yourself and you are learning to master your own emotions and responses, you'll find that you have more control over what is happening around you. Life will become less chaotic and more focused in your chosen direction. There will still be problems, but you are now armed with the knowledge to deal with them quickly and are developing problem-solving skills. You'll also procrastinate less as you get used to making decisions. You are no longer just a spectator watching life happen to you; you can influence the outcome. It's like blogger and motivational speaker Israelmore Ayivor says, "You cannot score a goal when sitting on the bench. To do so, you have to dress up and enter the game."

8

MAINTAINING YOUR HEALTH

Caring about yourself is not being selfish or self-indulgent – it is essential. You get only one life and body, so it needs to be looked after.

Katie Reed, author, speaker, and mental health advocate, says, *"Self-care is giving the world the best of you instead of what's left of you."*

So how do you look after yourself?

The best treatment for general physical and mental health is prevention.

- *Eat well* – Choose meals with a lot of vegetables, whole grains, and quality protein. Add some fruits in a variety of colors. Keep your sugar and salt intake low, and choose unsaturated fats.

- *Keep active* - 30 minutes of physical exercise at least three times per week is the minimum. You can walk briskly, run, swim, shoot hoops, play sports, or go to a gym.
- *Avoid harmful substances* – Well done if you have never started smoking or taking drugs, you'll never have to battle to quit. These substances are known to erode your body and your brain and cause problems. Don't take them. If you do, get help to quit.
- *Protect yourself* – Wear a safety belt when traveling by car and a helmet when riding a bicycle or motorbike. Injuries can have long-lasting effects on your body, so try to avoid them.
- Always use protection to avoid sexually transmitted diseases.
- Use sunscreen with a protection factor of at least 30 if you are in direct sunlight. If you work in the direct sun every day, increase this to factor 50.
- *Sleep peacefully* – Your body needs to recharge and regenerate, which takes about 7 hours of good quality sleep. To help achieve this, you need a quiet, dark, comfortable environment without blue light from electronic devices or digestive action from heavy meals or drinks.
- *Drink well* – Lots of water helps your body function nicely. Avoid sugary, carbonated, and alcoholic drinks, or only drink them in small quantities.

- *Help with hygiene* – Keeping your body and hair clean by bathing or showering daily and brushing your teeth in the morning and at night will keep you free of germs. This also applies to keeping your home and immediate work environment clean too.
- *Keep your weight regular* – You can check many charts to see your weight parameters for your age, height, and body type. Obesity can lead to severe health conditions such as high blood pressure and diabetes.

Even though you are careful about how you treat your body and you look after yourself, there may be times when you do get sick and need to help your body recover.

OVER-THE-COUNTER MEDICINES

When you are young, your body should recover quickly so you can treat yourself with over-the-counter medicines bought at a pharmacy for mild illnesses such as a cold, allergy, or tummy upset. Ask the Pharmacist or assistant for guidance on what to buy. You should only take over-the-counter medicines as directed on the label. Taking more will not make it work more quickly or more effectively. If the medication you bought over the counter has not helped after three to five days or the pain or symptoms increase rapidly or significantly, you should see a doctor.

Here are some terms that will be helpful:

Analgesic – is a mild pain killer for minor injuries, body aches, headaches, or toothache.

Antihistamine – can be taken to counteract an allergic reaction.

Antipyretic – will reduce a mild fever.

Decongestant – to clear a blocked nose.

Mucolytic – breaks down phlegm and will loosen a cough.

Muscle relaxant – used for period pains or tension in the neck and shoulders.

NSAIDs (Nonsteroidal anti-inflammatory drugs) – to reduce swelling or pain in joints or ligaments.

Did you know?

For many centuries people believed that chicken soup helped to cure a cold. Don't laugh; recent research has confirmed that chicken is rich in cysteine, an amino acid that helps to loosen mucus and unblock a nose. This enzyme is even more effective when spices are added to it.

On the morning of his interview, Michael woke up with a dry, painful throat and a headache. Postponing or canceling the appointment was not an option, as it would reduce his chances of getting the job he wanted. He left home earlier than planned and stopped at the pharmacy to get some over-the-counter medicine. By this stage, he had developed a cough as well. He chose antibacterial throat lozenges and a cough mixture. Fortunately, the assistant pointed out that the cough mixture would make him drowsy – something he could not afford while doing an interview. He told her he needed to be alert, and she recommended a different cough syrup. He was glad that he had talked to her. He went for the interview and got the job to start at the beginning of the following month.

Two days later, Michael was still coughing and began to get pains in his chest and run a fever. He went back to the chemist, but when he got there, the Pharmacist suggested that he go and see a doctor because his symptoms were worse. He made an appointment for the same day. The doctor said that he had taken the correct over-the-counter medicine but that the problem was more serious and prescribed antibiotics for bronchitis.

Top Tip

An infection usually only gets better when you take an antibiotic, but a virus needs patience and rest as it works out of your body. So how do you know if you have a virus or an infection?

A virus gives a low-grade temperature, but an infection will get your temperature soaring above 39 deg C.

Symptoms of infection will last longer until antibiotics are taken.

With a virus, you will see improvement each day. However, an infection will make you feel worse and worse as the days pass. This is a sign to seek medical assistance.

BASIC FIRST AID KIT

When setting up your own home, traveling, or living away from home, you should have a few general items to help with minor illnesses and injuries. Keep these in a waterproof container in an easy-to-reach place. Stock your first aid kit with the following:

For dressing wounds:

- *Antiseptic* lotion or cream
- Band-Aid or plasters in various sizes
- Elastic wrap bandage and adhesive tape or safety pins
- Sterile swabs
- Cotton wool and cotton-tipped swabs

Medications:

- Paracetamol and ibuprofen for pain and fever
- Imodium or Loperamide for diarrhea
- A laxative
- An antihistamine
- Throat lozenges
- Cold medicines

Other:

- Burn gel
- Cold pack (in the freezer)
- Disposable gloves
- Scissors; tweezers
- Hand sanitizer
- Thermometer

WHEN TO GO TO THE DOCTOR

Most mild illnesses and injuries can be dealt with at home with proper self-care. Still, sometimes it is necessary to see a doctor for a diagnosis and stronger medication or medical treatment. You should go to the doctor if:

Your symptoms get worse – If you develop additional symptoms or suddenly get worse, you should see a doctor. If the symptoms linger on and you are not seeing an improvement after about five days, it is best to get assessed.

You have a high fever – This is your body's way of fighting off illness, but if you can't get the fever to reduce in 48 hours, it indicates that your body is not coping and needs help.

You have lost weight – When you have not intentionally lost weight by going on a specific diet, you should see a doctor to assess what may be causing this.

You are short of breath – Being out of breath after an activity is regular, but if you are battling to get air and wheezing or out of breath while resting, you need to see a doctor.

You have chest pains – Chest pains can be caused by anything from indigestion or a mild chest infection to a heart attack, so it is always advisable to see a doctor to rule out anything serious.

Your vision is blurred – Any problems with your vision, from blurry to bright flashing lights, should be checked out.

You experience sudden or noticeable changes – Any unusual changes in your body that are not normal growth development should be checked by a doctor. These would be a change in size or color of a mole or patch of skin, frequency in visits to the toilet, frequency or intensity of your period, etc.

You have injured your head – A severe knock to the head due to a fall or accident, even if there is no confusion or dizziness, should always be checked by the doctor to rule out a concussion.

You have an unusual reaction – If you are taking a new or increased dose of medication and have a reaction, or have had a surgical procedure and notice a decline in your health or condition of the wound, you should visit the doctor.

Other reasons to see the doctor

Mental health is as important as physical health. Sometimes, when there are many big changes to cope with all at the same time or ongoing stress, you could get depressed. This may be made even worse if you are lonely or feeling overwhelmed. If you are feeling any of these symptoms, please see a doctor or contact one of the numbers below for help.

- You easily get angry over things that never used to bother you
- You have feelings of hopelessness
- You feel empty or numb
- You often cry for no apparent reason
- You are no longer interested in hobbies or sports that you were passionate about
- You constantly blame yourself or feel guilty
- You just want to be left alone to sleep all the time
- You have lost your appetite and don't want to eat
- You have trouble concentrating and focusing on work or your studies
- You have frequent thoughts of dying or committing suicide
- Your family has a history of mental health issues as well as feeling any of the above.

Please do not battle alone - there is help around the clock. Besides many online options to get immediate help, you can also call:

In the US - 1-(800)-662-HELP (4357)

In the UK - 0031-343556400 or Text YM to 85258

HEALTH INSURANCE

The basic concept of insurance is that many people pay a small amount of money (premium) every month into a fund so that when a few people have a large expense, money is available to assist.

There is no penalty in the USA for not having health insurance. There are two types of insurance – through private companies or public insurance providers such as Medicare, Medicaid, and the Children's Health Insurance Program. There are four different types of private insurance plans:

Health Maintenance Organization (HMO) plans: Except in an emergency, there may be limitations on which networks you can use. You are also tied into using the HMO in the area in which you live.

Preferred Provider Organization (PPO) plans: Usually, these plans contract to a network of service providers you will have to use, and you could pay less for this. But, additional costs will be charged if you use service providers outside the preferred network.

Point of Service Plans (POS): With these plans, you will need a referral from a primary doctor before you can see a specialist.

Exclusive Provider Organization (EPO) plans: These are managed care plans with costs covered only if you use the network providers (except in an emergency).

In the UK, there is a publicly funded healthcare system. The National Health Service (NHS) is provided through taxes and is available to the public at no cost. Private healthcare insurance is also available, and it can be useful to have for the following reasons:

- You will have priority access to treatment by medical professionals in private practice.
- Although the public health care system makes every effort to attend to patients quickly, it is overloaded. So private insurance will allow you to book directly with your choice of a private hospital, thereby shortening the waiting period.
- Instead of sharing a ward with other patients, you will be treated in your own room, giving you and your family privacy.
- Your health insurance provider will pay your bill directly to the hospital, ensuring that you are not out of pocket and reducing the need to self-fund expensive treatment.
- It gives you access to treatment and medicine that may not be available to the NHS network due to cost or NICE (National Institute for Health and Clinical Excellence) regulations.

- You can choose your specialist after researching or getting recommendations from family or friends.

Choosing healthcare insurance

Check with your employer

Some companies offer group healthcare insurance which means that your monthly premium is subsidized or you get a cheaper rate. At some companies, it is compulsory to join the insurance service provider that they have chosen. If you have a choice of whether to join, make sure that you understand the benefits and if there are any exclusions before signing up.

Weigh up your needs

If you are usually a healthy person, you will probably be able to pay for any care you occasionally need. However, it is always best to be prepared for a worst-case scenario. However, if you are often ill or have a chronic illness, you will probably need some assistance and should consider taking out health insurance. When your job or hobby puts you at a high risk of injuries such as logging, roof repairs, trucking, paragliding, parachuting, and so on, you should consider having health insurance.

Compare network providers

Establish whether the insurance provider gives you a choice of a healthcare provider or if you have to use a specific network only. If this is the case, research the network thoroughly to ensure that there are facilities near your home or work and that the care is good. Reading reviews is always a good idea.

Check the benefits

You always get what you pay for. Ensure that the benefits you need are listed under the minimum benefits covered and paid for. For example, if you like extreme sports and plan to go skiing for your next holiday, but the health insurance you are considering excludes sporting accidents, it is not the right insurance for you.

Disclose all necessary information

Some insurance providers have a waiting period for existing conditions. It is essential to let the provider know of any chronic illnesses that you have been diagnosed with. Although they may still give you a waiting period before you can claim, they may refuse all future claims if you do not disclose this information.

Affordability

Expensive healthcare insurance that you may or may not use is not advisable. Instead, take out a basic plan that only covers big events rather than paying a lot for benefits you are never likely to use.

DEALING WITH MEDICAL EMERGENCIES

It may happen that you or someone you know has a medical emergency, and initially, you are the only person that can help.

1. *Don't panic* – If you remain calm, you can think clearly and take control of the situation until qualified medical personnel can help.
2. *Breathe* – Take a deep breath and check if the patient is breathing. If the patient is not breathing, you need to call for help and start CPR, which is described further in this chapter.
3. *Assess the situation* – Make sure there is no further danger to yourself or the patient. If there is danger, such as a fire or oncoming traffic, get the patient to a safer place, moving them as gently and as little as possible. Do not move the patient if there is no further immediate threat.
4. *Call for help* – Save the number for local emergency services on your phone today so that you have it if necessary. When you place a call, you need to be able to give some details, such as the address, what symptoms you observe, and what has happened. It is a good idea to remain on the call so that a medic can talk you through how to stop severe bleeds or do CPR. Switch your phone to a loudspeaker, so you have both hands available to work.

5. *Support* – Talk to the patient if they are conscious to let them know that help is on its way and to keep them conscious.

BASIC FIRST AID

Cardio-pulmonary resuscitation is used when a patient is not breathing. Work as gently as possible with unconscious patients to avoid further injury.

- Ensure that nothing is blocking the airway. Use your fingers to clear away anything that is in the mouth.
- Moving the neck and head as little as possible, gently roll the patient onto their back and tip the head back slightly to open the airway. If you have a sterile mouthpiece, insert it securely into the patient's mouth.
- Place the base of your hand (the section just before the wrist) in the middle of the patient's chest, with your other hand on top.
- With your weight directly over your hands, push down hard to a depth of about two inches (five cm) and then release by lifting your weight off. This is one compression. Continue doing thirty compressions at a pace of two per second.
- If you have a mouthpiece, you can do two rescue breaths after every thirty compressions. Pinch the nose closed to make a tight seal and breathe into the

mouthpiece with a firm and steady breath to make the chest rise. Do two steady breaths, then another thirty compressions.

- Continue until medical help arrives or the patient wakes up completely.

For children younger than eight, use only one hand to a depth of about one inch (2,5 cm) for compressions. For babies, use only two *fingers*.

Top Tip

Each country has its own emergency number, which can be found on the internet. When traveling, always make sure to find out the local emergency number and save it on your phone.

United States of America – 911
United Kingdom – 999
Other common numbers – 117, 10111, 112, 122

Bleeding

Firstly, assess how bad the bleeding is. A small trickle of blood can be dealt with efficiently by swabbing with an anti-septic liquid and covering it with a dressing. If there is a consistent pouring flow or bright red spurting blood, you must act quickly and deal with these wounds first.

Place an antiseptic or sterile swab over the wound and hold it in place with a bit of pressure. If no blood seeps through, secure it with a bandage. Never remove the swab to check, as you can interfere with the clotting process.

If you find that the swab quickly soaks through with more blood, place more swabs in position and try to raise the wound above the level of the head. Never use a tourniquet but allow the medic on the phone to talk you through finding a pressure point to help stop the bleeding. When blood no longer seeps through the additional swabs, bandage the wound.

Poisoning

Look around the area to find what substance could have been swallowed, as the hospital will need this information. If the patient is not breathing, start CPR but do NOT do rescue breaths even with a mouthpiece, as you may put yourself in danger too. Look for the following signs - the smell of chemicals around the nose or mouth, burn marks around the mouth, vomiting, difficulty breathing, confusion, or unresponsiveness.

Broken bones

Unless a bone has snapped in two and there is a big knob on the limb, it is difficult to tell if a bone is broken without an x-ray. Look for swelling or redness and ask the patient (if conscious) to tell you how intense the pain is on a scale of one to ten. The bone will likely be broken if numbness and pain worsen with movement. The bone should not be straightened but supported if you can gently slide a hard, firm flat item under it. Bandage without pressure to secure the support.

Burns or scalds

A burn is caused by dry heat, such as an iron or stove plate. A scald is caused by hot liquid, such as kettle steam or boiling water.

- Ensure the patient is removed from the heat source as quickly as possible.
- Take off clothing around the burn, careful not to tear the skin. If the clothing has stuck, leave it for a medical professional to deal with.
- Stop the burn with cool running water for about twenty to thirty minutes. Never use iced water, ice, or greasy substances like cream or butter.
- Ensure the patient is kept warm to prevent shock, but do not cover or irritate the burned area.
- Get the patient to a hospital as soon as possible if the burn is chemical, the skin is white or charred, or burns are on the face, neck, or joint.

Anaphylactic shock

This is a severe and life-threatening reaction to an allergen. The substances that most commonly cause a person to stop breathing are peanuts, shellfish, and bee stings. Usually, teenagers and adults know they are allergic to these substances and will avoid them. In severe cases, they may carry medication, and you will need to assist them by fetching it and dispensing it. Symptoms include being light-headed or faint, difficulty breathing, wheezing, severe swelling, and collapsing.

Your body can heal itself if you look after it, and you will mostly be able to treat yourself. Occasionally you may need the intervention of a doctor or trained medical professional. With the knowledge you have gained from this chapter, you will be able to help in an emergency and should not be afraid to do so. Some help is better than no help. Who knows, stopping a bleed or doing basic CPR may save a life.

CONCLUSION

Maya Angelou, a civil rights activist and world-famous writer, said, "I did then what I knew how to do. Now that I know better, I do better." After reading this book, her words should be ringing true for you.

Now you know better, you'll want to 'flex' as you intentionally take up the position of 'CEO' of your own life and start applying this information to real-life situations. So, let's look at how you've managed to 'glow up' over the eight chapters…

Shopping is a cinch as you approach it like a chef, using cooking utensils and equipment to save time when preparing delicious healthy meals. You're 'securing the bag' with an excellent job. Now all you need to do is keep track of where your 'guap' is going by following your budget carefully, focusing on what you need rather than what you want, and ensuring that your savings and investments allow you to still live your best life when you retire. Who would have thought that your fam would be checking with you about dress codes for events and how to launder, iron, fold and repair their clothes? Respect is what you've gained by keeping your home tidy and clean with the tips you read in this book. You even know how to get things fixed or whom to call to do it for you. Travel is efficient now that you know how to read timetables and negotiate routes and maps. Next, you'll consider buying your own car and getting health insurance - truly adult decisions. The decision-making skills you've learned are bound to help. You've become more comfortable interacting with colleagues at work and out-of-work social events, and soon you'll get up the courage to host your own party. You are clued up on how to stay safe from fraudsters by securing your passwords and using a VPN. Physically and mentally, you are in good shape from following the guidelines for looking after yourself and will be able to treat yourself for odd minor seasonal ills.

You'll find that as you develop into a responsible adult, putting the key themes of each chapter into practice, you will be taken seriously and given the respect you deserve.

So, if you haven't already done so, start putting the suggestions you've been given and start living your best life. Why not 'flex' your newly gained knowledge and leave an honest review on Amazon so that others leaving home for the first time can benefit from this information and won't be salty? You know, this book 'hits different.'

REFERENCES

Cooper, M (2022, January 3) *Healthy Bread Brands You Can Find in Any Grocery Store* TastingTable.https://www.tastingtable.com/719176/healthy-bread-brands-you-can-find-in-any-grocery-store/

Mendes, A (2022, October 28) *How to Clean A Blender* WikiHow https://www.wikihow.com/Clean-a-Blender

Elkus, G. (2021, July 21) *The Ultimate Guide to Picking only the Best Produce* Real Simple https://www.realsimple.com/food-recipes/shopping-storing/how-to-pick-produce

Gold, B (2020, August 3) *9 Smart Simple Ways to Save Money on Groceries* Real Simple https://www.realsimple.com/food-recipes/shopping-storing/food/how-to-save-money-on-groceries

Quilon, P (2022, June 19) *A Teenager Asked for Advice on Grocery Shopping for the First Time, and People Responded With Genuinely Excellent Tips* BuzzFeed https://www.buzzfeed.com/pernellquilon/first-time-grocery-shopping-tips

Barnet, H (2018, July 13) *24 Essential Cooking and Baking skills Your Teen Should Know* SheKnows https://www.sheknows.com/food-and-recipes/articles/1140231/cooking-skills-for-teens/

Regina, L (2022, August 2) *The Different Types of Kitchen Knives and Their Uses* HealthyKitchen 101 https://healthykitchen101.com/blog/types-of-kitchen-knives/

Giri, K (2022, January 13) *Why Every Student Should Own an Instant Pot* Varsity https://www.varsity.co.uk/sponsored/why-every-student-should-own-an-instant-pot

Collaboration of unknown Authors (2021, October 21) *How to Use a Hand Mixer* WikiHow https://www.wikihow.com/Use-a-Hand-Mixer

Braider, J (2016, June 30) *Cooking 101: Heat Levels and Cooking Speed* The Balanced Kitchen http://www.balancedkitchen.com/2016/06/cooking-101-heat-levels-and-cooking-speed/

Author unknown (2022, June 30) *Budgeting for Teens: 14 Tips For Growing Your Money Young* Intuit MintLife https://mint.intuit.com/blog/budgeting/budgeting-for-teens/

Pritchard, J (2022, June 1) *Get to Know the Parts of a Debit or Credit Card* The Balance https://www.thebalancemoney.com/parts-of-a-debit-or-credit-card-front-and-back-315489

Marquit, M (2022, January 15) *What is a Bank Statement* The Balance https://www.thebalancemoney.com/what-is-a-bank-statement-5092371

Author Unknown *What Types of Bank Accounts are There?* The Co-operative Bank https://www.co-operativebank.co.uk/tools-and-guides/current-accounts/what-types-of-bank-accounts-are-there/

Santelli, C (2022, September 8) *How to Buy Clothes That Fit* WikiHow https://www.wikihow.com/Buy-Clothes-That-Fit

Readers Digest Complete Guide to Sewing

Paudyal, N (2022, March 2) *The Ultimate Guide To Dress Codes: What to Wear For Every Occasion* LifeHack. https://www.lifehack.org/367501/the-ultimate-guide-dress-c odes-what-wear-for-every-occasion

Sullivan, D (2022, December 15) *6 Clothes-Folding Techniques That Save Closet and Drawer Space* The Spruce https://www.thespruce.com/folding-hacks-that-save-major-closet-and-drawer-space-3017373

Mirjan, A (2022, September 15) *How To Iron* WikiHow https://www.wikihow.life/Iron

Author Unknown *Going with the Flow: Gen Z v Millenials* Lunette https://www.lunette.com/blogs/news/going-with-the-flow-gen-z-vs-millennials

Danilowicz, M (2022, December 18) *How to Hand Sew a Hem* WikiHow https://www.wikihow.com/Hand-Sew-a-Hem

McLennan, T (2022, February 24) *How to pick the right Student Accommodation* The Uni Guide https://www.theuniguide.co.uk/advice/student-accommodation/how-to-pick-the-right-student-accommodation-for-you

Bieber, C.R. (2022, November 01) *7 Tips to Help You Pay Your Bills On Time* Credit Karma https://www.creditkarma.com/advice/i/tips-pay-bills-on-time

Gatchalian, B & Pina C (2022, January 27) *How to Clean Your House Quickly and Efficiently According to Experts* Woman's Day https://www.womansday.com/home/organizing-cleaning/tip s/a4055/a-quicker-way-to-clean-house-83178/

Atkins, A & Sullivan, C (2022, March 7) *50 Quick and Easy Cleaning Tips for Every Room in Your House* Woman's Day https://www.womansday.com/home/organizing-cleaning/tips/g2287/easy-cleaning-tips/

Author Unknown *The Five S's in 'Kaizen'.* Web Kaizen https://web-kaizen.com/kaizen/five-s-kaizen/

Speech To Change Your Life Today! Admiral McRaven "Make Your Bed" Motivational Words Of Wisdom https://news.utexas.edu/2014/05/16/mcraven-urges-graduates-to-find-courage-to-change-the-world/#:~:text=If%20you%20can't%20do,off%20by%20making%20your%20bed.

Glossary of Road Transport Terms Wikipedia https://en.wikipedia.org/wiki/Glossary_of_road_transport_terms#Rumble_strip

7 Essential Travel Safety Tips Nationwide https://www.nationwide.com/lc/resources/home/articles/travel-safety-tips

Karsten, M (2022, March 1) *25 Important Travel Safety Tips Everyone Should Know* Expert Vagabond https://expertvagabond.com/travel-safety-tips/

Lacivita, B (2022, September 22) *How to Change a Tire* Family Handyman https://www.familyhandyman.com/article/how-to-change-a-car-tire/

Tretina, K (2022, March 25) *What is Car Registration and Why Is It So Important?* Investopedia https://www.investopedia.com/what-is-car-registration-and-why-is-it-so-important-5185431#:~:text=In%20the%20U.S.%20car%20owners,your%20registration%20before%20it%20expires

Biggs, B & Pappas, S (2022, November 03) *Personality Traits & Personality Types: What Personality Type Are You?* LiveScience https://www.livescience.com/41313-personality-traits.html

Parenting Blog *An Introduction to the Four Temperaments* The Rose Garden https://therosegarden.us/blog/article:08-16-2009-12-00am-an-introduction-to-the-four-temperaments/

Unrestricted Access Worldwide ExpressVPN https://www.expressvpn.com/go/unrestricted-1

Author Unknown *Four Temperaments: Sanguine, Phlegmatic, Choleric, and Melancholic Personality Types* Psychologia https://psychologia.co/four-temperaments/

Author Unknown *Party Etiquette Tips for Hosts and Guests* Etiquette since 1922 https://emilypost.com/advice/general-entertaining

Leibowitz, R (2015, December 15) *Cyber Safety – Things to Know about Cyber Stalking* https://www.linkedin.com/pulse/cyber-safety-things-know-cyberstalking-rianette-leibowitz?trk=public_profile_article_view

Scott, E (2022, September 24) *Why It's Important to Apologize in Relationships* VeryWell Mind https://www.verywellmind.com/the-importance-of-apolo gizing-3144986

Top 10 Tips for Effective Workplace Communication Chrysos HR Solutions Limited https://www.chrysos.org.uk/blog/top-10-tips-for-effective-work place-communication

Indeed Editorial Team (2022, July 30) *Analytical Skills: Definition, Tips and Examples* Indeed https://in.indeed.com/career-advice/career-develop ment/analytical-skills#:~:text=You%20can%20make%20interpretations% 20based,of%20performance%20and%20financial%20data

Eason, B (2021, January 27) Self-Management Skills for a Messy World Betterup https://www.betterup.com/blog/self-management-skills-for-a-messy-world

Korn, M (2022, July 06) 10 Ways to Thrive As An Introvert in College Grown & Flown https://grownandflown.com/10-ways-an-introvert-can-thrive-college/

Korn, M (2020, September 15) *Students Give Best Advice On Coping With Loneli-ness in College* Grown & Flown https://grownandflown.com/students-grads-advice-overcome-loneliness-college/

Adebisi, J (2021, July 21) *Act Don't React: Take Full Control Of Your Life* Short-form https://www.shortform.com/blog/act-dont-react/

Evie (2017, June 4) *How to Mindfully Respond to Situations* Mindfully Evie https://mindfullyevie.com/mindfully-respond-situations/

Salters-Pedneault, K (2020, November 16) *Learning to Observe and Accept your Emotions* VeryWellMind https://www.verywellmind.com/emotional-acceptance-exerc ise-observing-your-emotions-425373

Understanding Over the Counter Medicines U.S Food and Drug Administration https://www.fda.gov/drugs/buying-using-medicine-safely/understand ing-over-counter-medicines

Author Unknown *Tips for Staying Healthy* UCSF Health https://www. ucsfhealth.org/education/tips-for-staying-healthy

Author Unknown *10 Signs You Should Go See The Doctor* Houston Methodist Leading Medicine https://www.houstonmethodist.org/articles/should-i-see-a-doctor/

Author Unknown *Foods To Eat And Avoid With The Flu* Medical News Today https://www.medicalnewstoday.com/articles/326306#foods-to-avoid

Ashford, K & Glover, L (2022, April 04) *How To Choose Health Insurance Your Step By Step Guide* Nerdwallet https://www.nerdwallet.com/article/health/choose-health-insurance

Yared-West, C (2021, September 05) *Five Common Medical Emergencies And What To Look Out For* LifeHealthcare https://www.lifehealthcare.co.za/news-and-info-hub/latest-news/five-common-medical-emergencies-and-what-to-look-out-for/

Printed in Great Britain
by Amazon

31578308R00119